Slow of Speech and Unclean Lips

Slow of Speech and Unclean Lips

Contemporary Images of Preaching Identity

Edited by

ROBERT STEPHEN REID

Foreword by Thomas G. Long

CASCADE *Books* • Eugene, Oregon

SLOW OF SPEECH AND UNCLEAN LIPS
Contemporary Images of Preaching Identity

Cascade Books
An Imprint of Wipf and Stock Publishers
199 W. 8th Ave., Suite 3
Eugene, OR 97401

www. wipfandstock.com

ISBN 13: 978-1-60608-521-9

Cataloging-in-Publication data:

Slow of speech and unclean lips: contemporary images of
preaching identity / Robert Stephen Reid, with a Foreword by Thomas
G. Long.

xx + 196 p. ; 23 cm. Includes bibliographical references and index.

ISBN 13: 978-1-60608-521-9

1. Preaching. 2. Rhetoric—Agency. 3. Preaching—United States.
4. Bible—Homiletical use. I. Reid, Robert Stephen. II. Long, Thomas G.
III. Title.

BV4211.3 S61 2010

Manufactured in the U.S.A.

An earlier version of Anna Carter Florence's essay, "Preacher as One
'Out of Your Mind,'" was originally published as "Out of Your Mind,"
Journal for Preachers 28.4 (2005) 36–39. Used by permission.

For Barbara Reid, MA, DWS
ordained to Christian ministry
December 7, 2008

Treasured spouse and partner in all my ventures.

May you find the means to discover
your own preaching trope
as you consider the possibilities suggested here.

Contents

Contributors

CHARLES L. CAMPBELL is Professor of Homiletics at Duke Divinity School, Durham, North Carolina. He is ordained in the Presbyterian Church (PCUSA) and was President of the Academy of Homiletics in 2008. His most recent book is *The Word before the Powers: An Ethic of Preaching* (Westminster John Knox, 2002).

ANNA CARTER FLORENCE is the Peter Marshall Associate Professor of Preaching at Columbia Theological Seminary in Decatur, Georgia. She is an ordained minister in the Presbyterian Church (PCUSA) and holds degrees from Yale University and Princeton Seminary. Her most recent book is *Preaching as Testimony* (Westminster John Knox, 2007).

LINCOLN E. GALLOWAY is Associate Professor of Homiletics at Claremont School of Theology, Claremont, California. He is from the Caribbean island of Montserrat and the Methodist Church in the Caribbean and the Americas. He is currently the pastor of Highgrove United Methodist Church in Riverside, California. He is convener of Bible and Hermeneutics Group for the Academy of Homiletics and his most recent book is *Freedom in the Gospel* (Peeters, 2004).

LUCY LIND HOGAN is Hugh Latimer Elderdice of Preaching and Worship at Wesley Theological Seminary in Washington,

DC. Ordained in the Episcopal Church, she has taught at Wesley since 1987. She is currently the co-president with Dr. Thomas Troeger of *Societas Homiletica*, the international homiletic academy. Her recent works include: *Graceful Speech: An Invitation to Preaching* (Westminster John Knox, 2006), and *Lenten Services* (Abingdon, 2009).

JAMES F. KAY is the Joe R. Engle Professor of Homiletics and Liturgics and director of the Joe R. Engle Institute of Preaching at Princeton Theological Seminary, Princeton, New Jersey. A minister of the Presbyterian Church (PCUSA), he is the editor of the journal *Theology Today*. His most recent book is *Preaching and Theology* (Chalice, 2007).

JOHN S. MCCLURE is the Charles G. Finney Professor of Homiletics and Chair of the Graduate Department of Religion, Vanderbilt Divinity School, Nashville, Tennessee. He is an ordained minister in the Presbyterian Church (PCUSA) and the editor of the journal *Homiletic*. His most recent book is *Preaching Words: 144 Key Terms in Homiletics* (Westminster John Knox, 2007)

ROBERT STEPHEN REID is Head of the Communication Department and Director of the Master of Communication degree program at the University of Dubuque, Dubuque, Iowa. He is ordained to the American Baptist Ministry (ABC/USA) and convener of the Rhetoric Working Group for the Academy of Homiletics. His most recent book is *The Four Voices of Preaching* (Brazos, 2006).

ANDRÉ RESNER is Professor of Homiletics and Church Worship, Chair of the Department of Pastoral Theology, and Director of the Preaching Institute at Hood Theological Seminary, Salisbury, North Carolina. He is a minister of the Presbyterian Church (PCUSA) and convener of the Pedagogy Working Group for the Academy of Homiletics. His most recent book is *Just Preaching: Prophetic Voices for Economic Justice* (Chalice, 2003).

Foreword

THOMAS G. LONG

A CCORDING TO the old joke, the only way for a church to keep the pastor's reserved parking space free of interlopers is to mark it with a sign, one that does not say "Clergy Parking" or "Reserved for the Pastor" but rather "If you park here, you have to preach." Underlying the punchline is the commonly held conviction that preaching is not a task a sober-minded layperson would freely undertake, no matter how attractive the perks. Unlike box seats at Wimbledon, front row center at a hit Broadway play, or the head of the line at the buffet table, the pulpit is considered a place no reasonable person would ever choose to occupy.

Why is this so? True, preaching is a form of public speaking, an ancient phobia with a near pandemic spread among the general populace. But the avoidance of the pulpit is caused by more than nerves; people who do manage to step up to microphones and bobble out a "few words" at PTA meetings, wedding receptions, Rotary Clubs, and karaoke bars nonetheless still give the pulpit wide berth. The fact that most people would rather be vaporized by a ray gun than be asked to preach a sermon transcends the simple fear of making a speech.

Perhaps, then, the widespread dread of the pulpit is the product of the deep discomfort many feel about speaking freely about religion, a notoriously controversial and taboo topic in polite conversation. People have a sixth sense, maybe, that standing up in a public place and talking about God while other people are supposed to sit and listen is a good way to get oneself scorned, parodied, disdained, subjected to withering critique, or even, if things get really out of hand, martyred. But this cannot be the whole truth either. There are many people who are quite willing to speak openly about their faith, in church school classrooms, small group settings, at the dinner table with friends, and even sometimes in public debate, but who nonetheless could never be coaxed into doing the same thing in a pulpit.

We get much closer to the truth, I think, when we bring into view what is happening in the event of preaching as a part of the larger context of worship. When one examines the texture of a service of worship, of the shape of the liturgy in other words, worship is quite clearly a piece of community theater in which the interaction between God and mere mortals is dramatically reenacted. Human beings have parts in this play and lines to speak, and likewise, God has a role and parts in the script. Viewed in this performative and theatrical way, the sermon is definitely one of those moments in the grand drama in which God acts and speaks through and with a human being. There are complexities and ambiguities galore, but the sermon is a "God moment," whatever that may mean.

No wonder, then, reasonable people instinctively shy away from the pulpit. It is a place where quite ordinary people are asked to do a quite extraordinary task, to speak not merely *about* God, but in some way to speak *for* God, *with* God, or even symbolically *in the role* of God. It is holy ground, on which flawed human clay is somehow molded and fired into a sacred chalice. If Rod Serling of 1960s television fame were still around, he could probably use his familiar mesmerizing voiceover to describe the pulpit, too, as "*a dimension as vast as space and as timeless as infinity . . . the middle ground between light and shadow, between science and superstition, and it lies between the pit of man's fears and the summit of his knowledge. This is the dimension of imagination. It is an area which we call the Twilight Zone.*"[1] In other words: if you park here, you have to preach, and if you preach, you have to don the mask of God.

James E. Dittes, who taught pastoral psychology for years at Yale, once observed that many ministers become irritated at parishioners who refuse to fill up the front pews and who insist upon sitting in the back of the church. However, such pastors, according to Dittes, badly misunderstand the significance of this behavior and are mistaken to be peevish about it. People prefer the back rows in church not because they are bored and uninterested in worship, Dittes argued. To the contrary, they crowd the rear because they intuit that something holy, mysterious, and even dangerous is happening up front, and they warily keep their distance. In other words, people don't want to sit in the front pews or, heaven forbid, climb the pulpit to preach for the same reason they don't want to walk through an electric power station wearing a blindfold and aluminum socks. Thus, it is not surprising to find in the Bible that those who preach are almost never volunteers; they are called, pressed, commanded, summoned, cajoled, dragged,

1. http://www.tvrage.com/The Twilight Zone.

perhaps even seduced into leaving the back pew and coming to "the front of the church" to prophesy and preach.

So what about those today who are called, pressed, and commanded into the pulpit? The fact that pastors regularly, vocationally, and peculiarly occupy this sacred and dangerous space and role may account not only for the fact that they often have reserved parking spaces but even more that they are almost always seen as a tad "odd." Even if they try hard to fit in by wearing day-glo clergy shirts, listening to punk rock on their IPods, and sporting vanity auto tags reading "RevMary" or "PastorBill," pastors possess an incurably liminal, in-between, social status. Remembering the black-suited Baptist ministers of his youth in small-town Pennsylvania, Harvey Cox wrote: "[The minister] was always something of an outsider, without cousins and uncles in town. He was *in*, but not *of*, our world, to paraphrase St. Paul . . . The preacher, even if he stayed five years, was always to some extent a stranger in a strange land. Maybe that gave him a little of the aura of transcendence or at least of the 'otherness' the representative of God must always signify, whether he likes it or not."[2]

Preachers are aware, of course, of this "aura of transcendence," this "otherness," and sometimes it makes their skin crawl and prompts them to shrink back from the fearful implications of standing in the holy space of the pulpit. The height is so dizzying; the abyss is so deep, so capable of evoking the instinctive fear of falling, the role so ill-fitting that preachers often whistle in the dark as they preach, pretending they are not where they truly are. Some crack lame jokes, others tell shaggy dog stories, the charming and personable ones do little soft shoe routines, some thrust the whole thing back to

2. Cox, *The Seduction of the Spirit*, 44.

the congregation ("divide into groups and discuss"), and still others puff up their chests and thunder out bromides or banal moralisms as if this were about their own moral authority, but everybody in the room—especially perhaps the preachers— knows that by minimizing the event these preachers are covering up their true calling, stepping away from the mystery that is preaching, shielding their eyes from the blaze of the burning bush that provoked them to do something so grand and foolish as to stand up there and preach in the first place.

What I am saying is that preaching, in essence, is a holy mystery, full of the implicit warnings to "stand back and take off your shoes" that such experiences of the *mysterium tremendum* carry, and this is why people who spend their days tightening bolts or sinking free throws or tapping out strokes on a keyboard would just as soon stay clear of it. The philosopher Gabriel Marcel famously distinguished between problems and mysteries. Problems, he said, are vexing questions that are difficult to address but able to be solved—such as how do we send a spacecraft to Mars? Or: how do we cure polio? We like problems, even hard ones, because at the end of the day, or the bottom of the notebook page, we can say, "There! That's done." Mysteries, however, are more frightening because they cannot be solved and we tend to lose ourselves in them; the more one knows about a mystery, the more enigmatic it becomes. Problems have logical and technical characteristics and can finally, through science and reason, be resolved, but mysteries have depths that can only be plumbed.

There are many problems about the practice of preaching, but finally preaching is not a problem but a mystery. The mystery is this: in preaching human words somehow get gathered up into the purposes and actions of God. How does this happen? We don't know; it is a mystery. That response is not ducking the question but facing it head on. As the essays in this volume show, some people have high views of this mystery and some have lower views, but almost everyone who has looked hard at the event of preaching acknowledges that we do have a mystery on our hands.

Because preaching is a mystery in which human word and divine word somehow interact, those who do faithfully answer the fearsome call to preach do not, by and large, enter the pulpit with crisp job descriptions, technical formulae, or precise blueprints for what they do. They show up instead with something like governing images, powerful metaphors for the preaching task that, while they do not specify what happens in the mystery of proclamation, do gather together the disparate pieces of this practice and guide those who engage in it. Some preachers see themselves as pastoral caregivers, others as gospel evangelists, still others as relational bridge builders, story tellers, social justice prophets, and the like. Implied in each of these images are not only directions for the content and delivery of sermons, but also claims about the theological nature of the preaching event.

In this book, eight of the most creative and thoughtful scholars in American homiletics take stabs at articulating what it means for a human being to walk into the "twilight zone" of the pulpit, and they do so by advancing what they view as compelling governing images for the preacher. By explicating these images, they *ipso facto* make theological statements about the nature of the preached word and make claims, implicit and explicit, about the relationship between human and divine agency in preaching.

Each of these essays can stand alone, and each represents a concise mapping of the homiletical terrain as seen by one author. However, it is when the chapters are read as an ensemble that they become even more interesting and revealing. The first impression that a reader of the whole volume takes away is that these authors, for all of their diversity and differences of opinion, are nevertheless tramping the same ground and working off common, if sometimes unstated, assumptions. Like scientists offering up opinions about the age and origin of a large meteorite that has just cratered into a Kansas wheat field, the homileticians in this book may bicker about this or that, but they are unanimous that something has happened out there and that they are gazing at the same dramatic phenomenon.

In the 1940s, the legendary teacher of preaching Halford Luccock described what he called a "jewel sermon," where the preacher takes a single idea and turns it in the light, "allowing different facets to catch the light and throw it into different realms of experience."[3] Taken as a whole, this book is a sort of "jewel sermon" in which all of the authors share a conviction that preaching is a mysterious and theologically pregnant event, but each of them, in turn, shines the light on a single facet of the whole.

Second, while each of the images advanced here is, presumably, something that the author would set forth as central and essential to preaching, there is, nevertheless, a sense of correction about each of the essays. The authors aren't merely making observations about preaching; they are trying to reform the practice. In short, each of the authors' images—whether it be James Kay's "Messenger of Hope,"

3. Luccock, *In the Minister's Workshop*, 137.

Chuck Campbell's "Ridiculous Person," Lucy Lind Hogan's preacher as "Lover," and the other images described in these pages—represents something the author not only finds crucial but also finds missing to a certain degree from the pulpit today. As such, there is in each chapter not only a portrait of what preaching should be but also a quarrel with what preaching, run aground in the shallows of American culture, has become.

It would be a misuse of this book if readers thought of these eight proposed governing images as interchangeable identities, like a trunk full of Halloween costumes ready for the preacher to try on, one after the other. Rather, this volume is an invitation to take this collection of essays in hand, like a jewel, and to turn them in the reader's imagination, receiving the flashes of light that reflect from each. By doing so, the reader will not "solve" the problems of the pulpit but will instead move more deeply and more boldly into preaching's profound mysteries.

Introduction

Robert Stephen Reid

T<small>HE</small> <small>ESSAYS</small> in this volume began as contributions to the Rhetoric Working Group for the 2007 meeting of the Academy of Homiletics, November 29 through December 1, 2007, held in Minneapolis, Minnesota. An earlier version of my essay and Chuck Campbell's essay[1] was included in the materials provided to Academy participants and discussed in the first working group session. The remaining essays were shared as eight minute briefs for a panel titled "'Slow of Speech and Unclean Lips': Homiletic Agency Re-imagined for a Generation of Disillusioned Ironists and Other Wary Seekers." My friend and occasional co-author, Lucy Hogan, wrote to me that she thought raising issues about agency may work as a panel title for the Academy working groups, but as a title for a book it lacked a certain cache. She said, "Save explanations about agency for the 'Introduction,' Bob." Lucy is usually right about these things.

In fact, she was the one who originally come up with the images of Moses claiming to be slow of speech (Exod

1. Professor Campbell's essay is a revised version of his Inaugural Address originally delivered when he assumed the Peter Marshall Chair of Homiletics, Columbia Theological Seminary, March 29, 2005.

4:10–13) and of Isaiah claiming to have unclean lips (Isa 6:1–10)—thanks again for the title Lucy. So I decided that it would be best to stay with the phrase of "Contemporary Images of Preaching" for the book's subtitle even though my real interest was to invite homileticians to share their own preaching tropes that quite naturally reveal what they believe about the nature of agency in preaching.

WHY CONSIDER ISSUES OF AGENCY IN PREACHING?

A few words on the idea of agency as an issue in homiletics may be helpful at this point. This collection of essays addresses the theological question of the relationship between the human and the Divine in preaching. I invited several homileticians to identify the trope, the imaginative figure of thought which best captures what they believe they are "up to" in preaching. This kind of reflection can speak to preachers and students of preaching who struggle in the effort to realize some of the assumptions they bring into the pulpit when they preach. It responds to the question of "How should I understand my role as one who preaches?" The essayists have been asked to fill in the blank "Preacher as . . ." in ways that explore the issue of agency as identity in the pulpit.

While the concept of *agency* may be new language for some readers, the question about the relationship between the human and the divine in preaching is not. Historically, people who have risen to the occasion to speak of faith for their generation have been keenly aware of their own limitations. They question "Who am I to speak for God?" The tension is revealed when we think of preaching Word of God.

What does that phrase mean for you? If you choose not to capitalize "word," the inference tends to reflect more the conception of scripture as "word of God." It places the emphasis on the preacher's task of interpreting scripture. On the other hand, if we think of preaching as capital "W" Word of God, that places the emphasis on how preaching can become God made present.

There are a variety of theological perspectives that explore how a preacher views scripture, revelation, and his or her own identity in preaching. Each perspective implies something about how that preacher would view agency—the relationship between the work of God, the work of the preacher, and what can occur efficaciously as a result of the act of preaching. For example, Mark Noll identifies the position of traditional evangelical scholarship on the question of the relationship between preaching and scripture by noting that, "When examining the evangelical study of Scripture, everything hinges upon a recognition that the evangelical community considers the Bible the very Word of God."[2] When one preaches the Word of God out of this perspective, which is to say "preaches the Bible," it tends to be an act that serves as an interpretative translation of what the preacher believes to be the implications of Scripture. It is the proclamation of this interpretation of the text that makes possible the efficacious work of the Holy Spirit. Revelation in this perspective is equated with the words of the Bible.

Other homileticians view preaching as "an event of encounter with God that leaves the congregation with stron-

---

2. Noll, *Between Faith and Criticism,* 6. This applies to other traditional approaches that view preaching as translation of meaning.

ger and deeper faith commitment to doing God's work."[3]
Preaching is Word of God in this perspective when it "coheres
with the biblical witness."[4] This view of revelation correlates
the eventfulness of human preaching and the choice of God
to be existentially encountered as the means by which people
can "meet God."[5]

Other homileticians, especially those deeply influenced
by the New Homiletic, view preaching as a means of experiencing the Christ event anew, where contemporary proclamation
of Jesus and the Gospel functions as a Word event in which
the intentions of God in Christ can be efficaciously apprehended by those who hear this preaching. Revelation in this
perspective is equated, not with what the words of Scripture
say, but with what the language of preaching, aligned with the
performative intentions of scripture *can do*.[6]

Yet other homileticians find that there is no authentic
proclamation of the gospel apart from preaching's social and
political relevance to transform a community of people to
participate in the emancipatory work of God. Preaching is
to be an imaginative, figural and intra-textual exploration of
concerns revealed in Scripture and culture.[7] Revelation in this
perspective is equated with the power of the biblical narratives and the apostolic letters preached to form emancipatory
communities of faith.

3. This is part of Wilson's definition of preaching in *The Practice of Preaching*, 21.

4. Farris, *Preaching that Matters*, 7.

5. Wilson, *The Practice of Preaching*, 21.

6. Randolph, *Renewal* (1969), vii; Reid, "Commentary," 113.

7. Campbell, *Preaching Jesus*, 250–57.

And still other homileticians believe that the illumination of the Holy Spirit alone is what makes the work of grace efficaciously possible—it is one of the means by which we are claimed by God. Preachers serve as provisional heralds of promise engaging in an action that "*God* has commanded and blessed."[8] These homileticians reject assumptions that would emphasize the work of the preacher as somehow evoking the presence of God through an effective use of language. Revelation in this perspective distinguishes the true revelatory witness, which is Jesus Christ, from the Bible, which is only a witness to that revelation.

As you read across these different theologies of preaching can you see how questions of agency and authority may differ for different preachers?[9] My hope is that questions arise:

- How do I understand the relationship between preaching and the Bible?

- What do I believe can happen through preaching?

- How much of what happens in preaching is the work of God?

8. Barth, *Homiletics* 72.

9. For explorations of these theologies in greater depth see Reid, *The Four Voices of Preaching*. Five options are suggested here. The first three correlate with the Teaching, Encouraging, and Sage Voices in my *map* of contemporary homiletic theory and practice. The final two options I depict are intended to be suggestive of post-liberal and neo-Barthian perspectives that function as specific versions of what I term the Testifying Voice in preaching. For other discussions that array contemporary homiletic theory and practice see Kay, "Theology of Proclamation," 493–98; Kay, *Preaching and Theology*; Wilson, *Preaching and Homiletical Theory*; and Long, "Authority," 440–44.

- How much of what happens might be a response to my efforts as a preacher to shape an appropriate or adequate message for those who gather to hear?

Such questions raise issues of agency worth considering.

WHY CONSIDER TROPES OF PREACHING?

My use of the word *trope* is likely more unusual for readers than use of the word *agency*. I am using the word to identify the often unacknowledged mental model we take on, like a mantle, when we step to the pulpit to preach. A *trope of thought*, unlike a *figure of speech*, functions as a way of thinking and reasoning drawn from one domain of knowledge and applied to arrive at understanding of another domain. Unlike a simple metaphor, which an individual usually is aware of using, a *trope of thought* can entail whole ways of knowing and assumptions that may be otherwise unexamined. Yet the person depends on that trope as a way of knowing that regularly frames what is said.

In the first half of the twentieth century the philosopher of language use, Kenneth Burke, actually transformed rhetorical thought by arguing that there were "Four Master Tropes" (metaphor, metonymy, synecdoche, and irony) which constitute the basis upon which humans are able to discover and describe everything that counts as truth.[10] We are accustomed to thinking about metaphor in this manner, but likely less familiar with the idea that irony functions in the same

---

10. Burke, *Grammar of Motives*, 503–17. For a helpful essay that explores the implications of the idea that there are four master tropes in human thought, see Tell, "Burke's Encounter with Ransom," 33–54.

way.[11] Yet many young people today find the ironic comedy of *The Daily Show*'s Jon Stewart or Stephen Colbert's *Colbert Report*, an approach to the news that skewers assumptions about what counts as truth, to be more truthful than standard news show that purport to report facts. This is irony doing its work as a master trope of understanding—as a way of apprehending the world. In this sense it is a bit disingenuous that the comedians want to label what they do as "fake" news. The problem is that they are using satire and irony to reveal the foibles of what counts as "real" news. And by engaging viewers with this ironic mental model of what counts as news, some viewers tend to trust the credibility of the comedians more than many other news pundits and commentators.[12]

Communication theorist John S. Nelson explains how simple tropes function in the following manner: "In ancient Greek . . . *tropos* means 'turn.' Figures of speech, experience, and endeavor are the turns we trace in apprehending the world. They are the movements that we enact when persuading ourselves and others. When these figures become utterly familiar, we take them to be the very character of our language: We literalize them."[13] When we literalize our figures we

11. For his part Burke would not be surprised with the recent success of comedians like Jon Stewart, Stephen Colbert, or to a lesser degree the late night comedians, as political pundits. Irony has always been a master trope. When Jon Stewart becomes a more trusted source for the news than ABC, NBC, CBS, FOX, or CNN, it may be that his use of irony as a means of drawing attention to behaviors has become a way of bringing truth to light for listeners who have grown suspicious that other news sources have become traduced by their own concern for access, their owner's business interests, or some other inhibiting concern.

12. Cf. Journalist Bill Moyers' interview with Jon Stewart available at http://www.pbs.org/now/transcript/transcript_stewart.html.

13. Nelson, *Tropes of Politics*, 28.

often become unaware that they constrain the way we look at the world and even constrain the identity we assume when we step to the pulpit. Eventually a simple trope may become a comprehensive trope of thought. Much more than a turn of speech or an embellishment that adds insight, a trope of thought can control an entire orientation to a way of knowing and understanding.

This notion of a trope of thought is at the heart of difference we bring to understanding our own preaching identity. Getting at these tropes is what I had in mind when I asked Anna Carter Florence,[14] Lincoln Galloway, Lucy Lind Hogan, James F. Kay, John McClure, and André Resner if they would give their answer to the question "Preacher as . . ." for the Academy panel. In my instructions to them I provided some examples of what I meant by a trope that functions as an identity in preaching. These examples arose from a prior conversation with John McClure. John is usually right about these things. Together he and I brainstormed that tropes of preaching might include images of "Preacher as":

- "Herald," who represents the message of another
- "Witness" torn from oneself by something wholly other, that claims one's life and so one's testimony (whether in the church courts or not)
- "Fool," wandering the streets preaching to principalities and powers rather than a specific audience

14. A version of this sermon was originally preached at the Festival of Homiletics, Washington D.C., May 19, 2004, and subsequently published in *The Journal for Preachers* 28.4 (2005) 36–39.

- "Roundtable Host," whose table conversation and meal is not his or her own
- "Supplicant," like the woman who anointed Jesus' feet,
- "Oracular Prophet," like the woman of Endor, or Joseph, who passively *divines* the ephod or dream— a kind of pre-runner to the clairvoyant *namer of grace,*
- "Ethical Prophet," whose identity and ethical vision is eschatological and whose agency is therefore entirely subsumed by desire to live into God's future.

In each instance, because preaching is in some sense God's activity, the agency of the preacher is according to McClure, 'under erasure.'[15] The degree of that erasure is clearly at issue in the essays of this volume.

FROM CONFERENCE TO BOOK

Thus, six homileticians in all were asked to think about the storied or theological manner in which either Biblical images or images from the traditions of the faith have shaped how they understand their call to speak on God's behalf. The basic question I posed to the participants was "*How is preaching both the work of God and yet also a function of the individual's own person and identity? What is the role of human agency in the divine-human dance called preaching?*"[16] It was under-

15. If this idea of communicating "under erasure" as a description of a person who speaks as "one *who is ultimately an approach to another*" is new to you see McClure, *Otherwise Preaching,* 19–26.

16. Notice my metaphor of "dance" tends to represent more of a view of double agency as a dialectical engagement, which is a different view

stood that their proposal of a trope of preaching was not to be viewed as exhaustive of their preaching identity. It was also clearly understood that none of the panelists were expected to arrive at the right metaphor/image/story/trope for preaching. Confessional differences as well as theological differences in our visions of appropriate tropes were respected.

The panel was held for one of the largest gatherings of any working group of the Academy in recent years. As will become evident in your reading of the essays that emerged from the event there was agreement on subject matter but wide divergence in styles of response. Some essayists composed their contribution in a highly personal manner while others adopted the voice of presenting reasoned argument. Some essayists adopted a sermonic style of composition, others adopted the style of an oral lecture, and still others chose to write in a manner that engages and advances theory for the discipline of homiletics. All of these stylistic differences were welcomed as writers revealed their tropes. Form tells us as much about the identity of the one who speaks or writes as does the content of what he or she shares.

What remains consistent across the presentations is a wonderful engagement that reveals a remarkable diversity of possible preaching identities. Of course there are many other identities. Perhaps you have already begun to think of the identity that shapes your own preaching. After reading the essays here, you may want to take time to explore the theological and the rhetorical dimensions of the trope that controls your own preaching identity. Would you simply adopt one of these tropes in this collection or do you have a new image to

of agency than John's use of "erasure" as a view of witness engaged in a "tearing up of itself on behalf of the other"; ibid., 25.

share or a fresh way to share a trope identified here? In what ways does this trope provide a set of rails that release you in preaching? Are there ways this trope constrains you and-or keeps you from going places that you might otherwise traverse? Are there ways that knowing what your trope is frees you to explore new corners of this identity? What does your trope reveal about who God is and how God acts?

This exercise will not only change how you preach, it will increase your ability to respond with clarity to the question, "What do I hope will happen as a result of people having heard what I have shared?" You may even want to ask, "What might God hope will happen as a result of people having heard this witness?"

I thank each of the essayists for their exceptional work in bringing this project to fruition. I also thank Tom Long for his preface. The title of Professor Long's durable textbook in homiletics, *The Witness of Preaching*, provides its readers with his preferred trope for "Preacher as . . ." In fact, he provides an essay length exposition of the value of this trope in his book that easily could have been an addition to this volume.[17] It seems fitting that having staked his claim about the person of the preacher, that he be given the opportunity to commend others who do the same.

I recall a seminary class in preaching three decades ago where I was assigned to read John Stott's *The Preacher's Portrait: Some New Testament Word Studies*. It was an exegetical exploration of different tropes of preaching found in the New Testament itself; Preacher as Steward, . . . as Herald, . . . as Witness, . . . as Father, and . . . as Servant. The strength of that book was its exploration and biblical exposition of images for

17. Long, *The Witness of Preaching*, 45–51.

preaching by Bible writers. I believe that the strength of the present volume is its invitation to people, who serve in professions where they are called upon to reflect and think about preaching, to ask themselves how theology and experience has functionally shaped their own trope of practice. In turn, they have generously shared a vision of the trope that not only shapes their approach to preaching, but the trope that influences their pedagogy of preaching as well. May reading the differences found here lead preachers and students of preaching to a similar task of discovering their own preferred trope of preaching. The Christian pulpit will be stronger for that theological work.

God be blessed.

—Pentecost 2009

1

Preacher as Messenger of Hope

JAMES F. KAY

*For Charles L. Bartow on his Retirement from
Princeton Theological Seminary*

AT THE 2007 annual meeting of the Academy of
Homiletics, Professor Robert Stephen Reid convened
a panel to discuss "the role of human agency in the divine-
human dance called preaching" through a "trope of homiletic
identity."[1] As this wording indicates, there is a tendency in
contemporary homiletics to move with dispatch to the agency
of the creature, either understood as the preacher or audience
(rhetoric) or as the sermonic or scriptural forms themselves
(poetics), even when considering "the divine-human dance
called preaching." Indeed, homiletics as taught today may
suggest that a sermon could be satisfactorily invented, constructed, delivered, and assessed without specific reference
to divine agency. If God appears in a homiletics textbook, it
may be as a perfunctory nod or as an appended afterthought

---

1. The panelists included Anna Carter Florence, Lincoln Galloway,
Lucy Lind Hogan, James F. Kay, John S. McClure, and André Resner Jr.

(perhaps postponed to a follow-up book) after all the heavy lifting has been done by some version of poetics or rhetoric. For this reason, finding an appropriate trope of "homiletic identity" may best begin by reflecting on our homiletic hesitations about God.

I

The silence of much contemporary homiletics about the God who speaks through the Scriptures, the sermon, and the preacher is not the result of our postmodern preoccupations; rather, it is the programmatic result of our modern ones. Paradoxically, the renewal of rhetoric and its systematic application to pulpit discourse by learned churchmen in the European Enlightenment bestowed legitimacy on homiletics as an academic discipline at the price of silencing discussion about the God who speaks. To recall the formulation of Johann Lorenz von Mosheim (1693–1755), signaling the switch from a theological to a rhetorical frame of reference, a sermon is no longer regarded in the first instance with reference to the Word of God, but, rather, "A sermon is a speech."[2] Even when the pious Archbishop François Fénelon (1651–1715) gives eloquent and explicit expression to divine agency in preaching in his *Dialogues sur L'Eloquence*, arguably the first modern rhetoric, it plays no significant material role in the rhetorical strategies he urges on preachers.[3]

---

2. von Mosheim, *Anweisung erbaulich zu predigen*, 11 (my translation). Mosheim's dictum serves as the programmatic motto for the rhetorically-based homiletics of Gert Otto.

3. Fénelon, *Dialogues on Eloquence*, 128–30.

Beginning with John Witherspoon (1723–1794), whose Princeton lectures on pulpit eloquence became integral to the first American rhetorical treatise, homiletics in America has generally taken rhetoric rather than theology for its basic frame of reference.[4] As the comprehensive *On the Preparation and Delivery of Sermons* by John A. Broadus (1827–1895) illustrates, by the end of the nineteenth century "the application of the principles of rhetoric to the art of preaching may be said to have been completed."[5] Declaring at the outset that "homiletics may be called a branch of rhetoric, or a kindred art," the living God makes no appearance in Broadus's influential textbook until page 504.[6] In the penultimate paragraph of this massive tome, two sentences finally surface indicating "our dependence for real success is on the Spirit of God" and "where one preaches the gospel, in reliance on God's blessing, he never preaches in vain."[7]

Significantly, the rhetorical turn taken by homiletics in the European Enlightenment occurred at the same time that supernaturalist accounts of divine agency, wherein God was seen as disrupting the laws of nature or violating the moral law which treats persons as valued ends in themselves, were rendered permanently problematic. One might summarize the Kantian strand in this story by saying that God was dislodged from direct agency in the world in favor of the rationally apprehended moral law which God authorizes.[8] God

4. Witherspoon, "Lectures on Eloquence," 231–318.

5. Hoshor, "American Contributions to Rhetorical Theory and Homiletics," 149.

6. Broadus, *On the Preparation and Delivery of Sermons*, 30.

7. Ibid., 504.

8. See Schneewind, *The Invention of Autonomy*, for a magisterial telling of the story summarized here.

is good because God adheres to the moral law to which he freely assents and thereby commends to his creatures. As the Creator, God only provides the necessary conditions (e.g., immortality) by which the moral law can be actualized by autonomously competent human agents. There is thus no need for any inner illumination or reorientation of the human will by an alleged Holy Spirit.

The resulting mantra of enlightened ethics is, "Yes, we can!" We are on our own and free to choose for ourselves. There are no more excuses. Just say "Yes" to what is wise, and just, and good; or conversely, "Just say, 'No!'" to what is foolish, unjust, and evil. Human beings need no saving in any traditional sense, just regular reminding of their duties by a morally earnest "bully pulpit": "The end of all preaching," Hugh Blair (1718–1800) declares to his Edinburgh students, "is to persuade men to become good. Every sermon, therefore, should be a persuasive oration."[9] Such requires a preacher, in Witherspoon's judgment, who is "*really*, *visibly*, and *eminently* holy."[10] Newly equipped with Locke's psychology about how "to bring it home," preaching was thus given over largely to ethical exhortation by the ethically eminent exhorter.

By deactivating divine agency, the goal was to activate human agency. The idea was to "tame" God, or at least our concept of God, in order to foster human accountability and responsibility. Unencumbered by claims for divine revelation in the preaching event, an autonomous and responsible rhetoric could now take charge of the pulpit. This is not to say that enlightened preachers no longer spoke of God. The *subject or topic* of God continued to make appearances in

9. Blair, *Lectures on Rhetoric and Belles Lettres*, 282.

10. Witherspoon, "Lectures on Eloquence," 297 (italics original).

sermons addressed to educated elites, but I have found little in the rhetorical theories stemming from the Enlightenment suggesting that God remains a Subject or active Agent in the preaching event itself. In place of the speaking God of the Scriptures, the ultimate sermonic Agent of the Reformers, God becomes "objectified" as the sermonic subject or topic of the preacher. "God" is a Christian doctrine which rhetoric receives or borrows from dogmatics or ethics for pulpit packaging and delivery. With the Enlightenment effectively banishing what was deemed either an all-controlling or un-controllable God from human affairs, rhetoric, with the best of Christian intentions, now steps on to the scene by showing preachers how to "take control" of their speechifying in service to their lofty rhetorical aims. Command and control are transferred from the Creator to the morally competent creature so that preaching becomes regarded as "a good person offering good reasons to good people."[11]

These Enlightenment perspectives, which remain influential to this day, are exemplified in the views of Harry Emerson Fosdick (1878–1969), the founding pastor of New York's Riverside Church. Fosdick declares:

> The preacher's business is not merely to discuss repentance but to persuade people to repent; not merely to debate the meaning and possibility of Christian faith, but to produce Christian faith in the lives of his listeners; not merely to talk about the available power of God to bring victory over trouble and temptation, but to send people out from their worship on Sunday with victory in their possession.

11. Hogan and Reid, *Connecting with the Congregation*, 91. For ways preachers are to "take control" of the communication event, see esp. 22, and, more recently, Reid, *The Four Voices of Preaching*, 26–30.

> A preacher's task is to create in his congregation the
> thing he is talking about.[12]

In accordance with his rhetorical commitments, all of the
predicates traditionally assigned by theology to God, including "to persuade folks to repent," "to produce Christian faith,"
and giving folks "victory over trouble and temptation," are
now transferred by Fosdick wholly to the preacher charged
with responsibility for authoring the "new creation." While
rightly indicating the eventfulness of proclamation, the saving outcomes sought by Fosdick now fall into the preacher's
portfolio—not God's. Whether Fosdick's remarks are read as
an expression of deism, or unwittingly, atheism or idolatry,
the titanic expectations he places on the preacher could cause
lesser mortals in the pulpit to sink beneath their weight.

If modernity's attempt to absorb preaching fully into its
rhetorical theories ironically turns homiletic practice away
from the living God, with further irony it also reduces rhetorical theory to speechlessness where the living God is still
remembered. George Campbell (1719–1796) in his *Philosophy
of Rhetoric* (1776), arguably the most comprehensive and
influential since antiquity, is forced to admit that if the over-
all aim of preaching is "the reformation of mankind," as he
himself holds, then the preacher "would need to be possessed
of oratory superior to human."[13] Surveying actual practice,
Campbell adds that achieving such repentance through
preaching "seems to bid defiance to the strongest efforts of
rhetorical genius."[14] Later, John Quincy Adams (1767–1848),

---

12. Fosdick, *The Living of These Days*, 99.

13. Campbell, *The Philosophy of Rhetoric*, 109.

14. Ibid., 111.

as the first Boylston Professor of Rhetoric at Harvard, also concedes with respect to the pulpit that rhetoric "entirely fails us."[15] Rhetorical canons, emerging from the ancient Greek polis, are not finally determinative for Christian preaching, presumably insofar as preaching's purposes require communication by God's own Word and Spirit. The God that Campbell and Adams conclude is necessary for preaching is not a God whom their rhetorical theories can actually allow. Their thought typifies the Enlightenment era when divine agency in the pulpit could not be seriously imagined by academic rhetoric or academic theology without seemingly impairing human agency.

II

Only when easy assumptions about human goodness and responsibility were silenced by the guns of World War I was divine agency in preaching seriously re-imagined. Karl Barth (1886–1968) rediscovered for a lost generation the speaking God of the Scriptures. He was soon joined by Rudolf Bultmann (1884–1976) and later, after World War II, the post-Bultmannian theologians of the New Hermeneutic. In differing ways, all these theologians of the Word took seriously the untamable God as the ultimate Agent of any sermon worthy of the name. Here is the Source of that "oratory superior to human" that George Campbell sought in vain but which can never be the "possession" of a preacher. Simply put, if the

15. Adams, *Lectures on Rhetoric and Oratory*, 1:322. Having recognized the difficulties, Adams still seeks "to apply the principles and method of Aristotle, so far as they can be applied, to this most recent species of public speaking," 1:324.

human words of a sermon are to become God's Word, then God must make them so. It is not in the preacher's power to speak God's Word, for the power of rhetoric is not inherently or necessarily the power of the gospel. Yet so compellingly did the post-Bultmannians correlate the agency of God's Word with that of human language (thanks to the linguistic turn signaled in Heideggerian poetics) that even a Barthian theologian like Hans Frei (1922–1988), could not resist transposing Karl Barth's *Church Dogmatics* into Erich Auerbach's (1892–1957) narratology in attempting a literary case for the agency of Jesus Christ. Frei's proposal, which figures prominently in homiletic postliberalism, is what Francesca Aran Murphy calls, "story Barthianism."[16]

Reading the Gospels as Auerbach's "realistic narratives," Frei crafts a composite literary Christology.[17] The character "Jesus" possesses a unique identity inferred from the incidents given in his story. The incident of the resurrection identifies him as one no longer subject to death. To omit this incident from the "identity description" of Jesus is thus impossible, for this incident, by literary convention, is integral to the character "Jesus" in the gospel narrative. To speak of Jesus always entails his narrative identity, for characterologically he *is* his story. Where his story is told, Jesus is claimed as present to us here and now as *actually* risen from the dead, since by definition Jesus would not be who he is without his resurrection. The present agency of Jesus Christ, or the power of God, is thereby "rendered" for readers (and presumably hearers) through

16. See Murphy, *God is Not a Story*.

17. See Frei, *The Identity of Jesus Christ*; and Auerbach, *Mimesis*. For the harnessing of Frei to homiletical theory, see Campbell, *Preaching Jesus*.

the formal properties of realistic narrative. What the church historically predicates of the Holy Spirit, Frei attributes to the autonomous rendering power of realistic narrative.

At the heart of this postliberal understanding of the scriptural text is the notion that the text is entirely self-referential; it is its own semiotic universe, and, it can therefore be understood and appropriated entirely on its own terms without any need for critical reflection on the world in which it arose, without any need for "translation" into the concepts and idioms of our contemporary world, and, more fatally for homiletics, without any recognition of God operating outside the gospel narrative as the ultimate Agent of his own rendering. Here we can recognize the influence of the New Criticism that reigned in American letters from its Yale headquarters in the 1940s and 1950s. For the New Critics, a poem is a self-contained and self-referential object. Eschewing interpretations based on reader response, authorial intentions, or traces in the text of its historical context (including the author's biography), New Critics perform close readings in the confidence that meaning lies within the poem and solely within the interaction of its own words, literary devices, and structured patterns of language. What is bracketed out of critical consideration is the world *behind* the text, as well as the world *in front of* the text, and, if I may be permitted a precritical spatial metaphor, the world *above* the text. This privileging of the organically united form and content of an "autonomous text" over its possible historical and contemporary contexts coincides nicely with dogmatic views of Scripture as self-referential and with Enlightenment views about interpretive "objectivity."[18]

18. For the influence of New Criticism on Frei, see Ellingsen, *The Integrity of Biblical Narrative*, 29–33.

Again to trace the Kantian thread in the story, told by Mark Alan Bowald as "the eclipsing and usurping of divine agency in Enlightenment epistemology," the paradigm sketched is that of a rational knower and a known object "immediately and immanently present to each other."[19] Moreover, for Kant independently achieved rational judgments possessing requisite objectivity, require a "moratorium on the influence of another agent on the knower," while the object itself is limited to what "can be perceived by human perception."[20] The result is to bracket out any antecedent grounds for appeal to divine agency as a factor in human knowledge. On these assumptions, the only agency operative in scriptural interpretation, insofar as it is an event of genuine knowledge, is human agency. With respect to Frei, the scriptural text "as the realized intention and expression of human authorial agency becomes the sole agent and container of its own meaning."[21] The text itself, purely as a creaturely form authored by human beings, is granted the power to render the identity and pres-

19. Bowald, *Rendering the Word in Theological Hermeneutics*, 1.

20. Ibid.

21. Ibid., 49, citing Frei, *Identity of Jesus Christ*, 87. Bowald argues that Frei, inconsistent with his narratological commitments, is forced to appeal to extra-textual divine agency to bridge the gap between the text and the reader. I remain skeptical that this is the case, but in any event Bowald judges the attempt a failure. In his later work, Frei correctively turns more from textual agency to the agency of its churchly-formed reader, but whether as autonomous text or as ecclesiastically circumscribed reader, it is the creature rather than the Creator who is the real acting agent of revelation. Despite its intention to overcome modernity, the poetics, hermeneutics, and homiletics of postliberalism remain as captive to Enlightenment assumptions as the rhetorical homiletics they seek to replace. For my own take on Frei, see *Preaching and Theology*, 108–20.

ence of Jesus Christ—and despite what the text itself might say about the continuing activity of the Triune God in the world outside the text. Whether one calls this epistemological move deistic, atheistic, or idolatrous, despite its intentions, it is difficult to reconcile it with the speaking God attested by the Scriptures.

If the identity and, hence, presence of God is "rendered" through the formal poetics of realistic narrative, why would one need Christian preaching? Why not just read these narratives or recite them? Why muck things up with exegesis, prayer, or preaching itself. The very fact that the church (and the synagogue before it) instituted the office of preacher (and rabbi), and not just those of lector (or cantor), suggests that the ever new situation into which preachers interpret the Scriptures requires taking account of the world into which the Scriptures arose, into which they are now read and proclaimed, and the new contexts into which they are addressed--and of which their human authors had no knowledge whatsoever. The Scriptures themselves indicate that God wills to speak anew through them today, that God is not trapped either in print or in the past. The God of the gospel attested by Scripture is therefore the most important contemporary living agent in the interpretive process and is not simply a character or object of literary inquiry confined to Bibleland. Every liturgical prayer for illumination and every epiclesis for the Holy Spirit to enliven the Word or enable our hearing of the Word makes this hermeneutical point as nothing else can.

At the time of the Reformation, Phillipp Melanchthon (1497–1560) rightly recognized that "faith does not mean merely knowing the story of Christ," since both the Devil and Judas knew that story very well. Faith "includes not only the story but also the promises and fruit of the promise."[22] That is to say, narrative agency cannot be equated with divine agency, or narrative presence with "real presence," without some accounting of "self-involvement" by the divine Agent in relation to contemporary hearers. Such "self-involvement" is not a property of "realistic narrative" as it is of "promises." Thus divine agency, that the theologies of the Word seek to honor in preaching, is not reachable by means of realistic narrative alone. While helping us to identify Jesus on the basis of a narrative reading of the gospels, and, thereby enabling us to "preach Jesus," Frei's postliberal poetics as "story Barthianism" cannot account for what the apostle Paul calls "the preaching of Christ" (cf. Rom 10:17), that is, the "preaching by Christ," that continues today in and through the preachers of the gospel.

The question thus before us en route to a trope of homiletic identity is whether we can envision preaching as an activity involving at least the double agency of the human preacher and God, who is the asymmetrically primary partner. (This is not to deny other multiple agencies exercised by listeners, as well as those of the "principalities and powers" that are potentially present in any communication event.) Despite the failure of Enlightenment-governed rhetoric and poetics to take adequate account of divine agency, that God uses human means to embody and proclaim the divine Word cautions against mirroring the theological reductionism of the Enlightenment by now denying either rhetoric or poet-

22. Melanchthon, *Melanchthon on Christian Doctrine*, 182.

ics their appropriate role in signifying the gospel.[23] For this reason, the Book of Hebrews holds special promise for contemporary homiletic theory. Here, we are given a rhetorically conscious scriptural witness to the God who speaks to us not only through Scripture, but through its sermonic exposition by representatives of the church.

III

While no exhaustive account of Hebrews is remotely attempted or intended here, some soundings from its pages as "one of the earliest extant Christian sermons" is instructive in sorting out divine-human agency, the role of rhetoric, and tropes of "homiletic identity."[24] Styling itself a "word of exhortation" (Heb 13:22), Hebrews is "a masterpiece of early Christian rhetorical homiletics," and, to use Aristotle's terminology, could be largely categorized as an "epideictic oration" in praise of the faithfulness of Jesus Christ.[25] Such rhetorical devices as antithesis (a contrast of ideas by parallel arrangement), paronomasia (word plays or puns), synkrisis (formal pairings of comparison or contrast), amplification (expanded statements), and euphonious alliteration are all present.

Nevertheless, this is not a scriptural instance of an a-theological baptism of rhetoric, for the message of the speaking God simultaneously modifies its conventions. As Craig Koester notes, while ancient orators typically began

23. For opposition to rhetoric along these lines see Owens, "Jesus Christ Is His Own Rhetoric!"; and Willimon, *Proclamation and Theology*.

24. Koester, "Hebrews, Rhetoric, and the Future of Humanity," 103.

25. Attridge, *The Epistle to the Hebrews*, 1 and 14.

their speeches by recounting what people had previously said about a topic, the exordium or introduction to Hebrews "shifts the level of discourse from human speech to divine speech by focusing on God."[26] Moreover, we do not have here any standard invoking of deities to assist the speaker, but rather the exordium "identifies God *as* the speaker":[27]

> Long ago God spoke to our ancestors in many and various ways by the prophets, but in these last days he has spoken to us by a Son, whom he appointed heir of all things, through whom he also created the worlds. He is the reflection of God's glory and the exact imprint of God's very being, and he sustains all things by his powerful word. (Heb 1:1–3a)

This introduction also reverses a rhetorical commonplace of the time, namely, that language had become debased and jargon-laden, the complaint of Philo and others. As Koester again notes, the preacher emphasizes the superiority of what God is saying *now*. "Many may have thought that human speech was degenerating, but God was not captive to the trend."[28] From the outset, a theological reframing by Hebrews of customary rhetorical conventions and convictions sounds a strong note of hope. Whatever the deplorable state of language, preaching, or the church itself cannot muzzle the speaking God who "has spoken *to us* by a Son." That this is proclaimed by a master wordsmith, who offers his sermonic rhetoric in service to the Word of God, cautions us against the notion, sometimes made in the name of piety, that

26. Koester, "Hebrews," 108.

27. Ibid.

28. Ibid., 109.

proclamation of this Word is most honored through a studied ignorance of the art of public speaking.

God's Word finds expression in Scripture, both as direct address to human beings and also, if I may be permitted an anachronism, as God's own Word directed within and among the persons of the Trinity which human beings overhear through Scripture.[29] Nevertheless, these instances of divine speech are not confined to Scripture as a rhetorical artifact of the past; rather they can be re-released in the words of subsequent human preachers. The Holy Spirit, who speaks "today" through the expounded Scriptures (3:7), continues to speak through the Scriptures' expositors (3:7—4:13). For example, God reiterates his judgment against the disobedience recounted in Numbers 14:20–23, "saying through David much later" (4:7) in Psalm 95, and now in the preacher's sermon on that Psalm itself, "Today, if you hear his voice, do not harden your hearts," lest the listeners of the Hebrews homily, too, "not enter my rest" (4:5). Through preaching, Scripture is interpreted by Scripture into a new situation that neither Moses nor David could have foreseen, and that interpretation is itself styled, "God's Word." We see this in Hebrews 13:7 where listeners are exhorted to "remember your leaders, those who spoke the Word of God to you; consider the outcome

29. Hebrews consistently quotes Scripture as spoken and not simply written, using some form of *legein* (rather than *gegraphtai*) to introduce citations. Of 35 quotations, some identify God (23), Jesus (4), or the Holy Spirit (4) as the speaker. I am grateful to Amy L. B. Pealer, PhD candidate at Princeton Theological Seminary, for this statistical summary. Sometimes these words are incorporated into sermonic discourse and thereby addressed to contemporary hearers or readers; sometimes, to speak retrospectively, these words are directed within the Triune community of divine persons. I am grateful to Richard B. Hays on this latter point.

of their way of life, and imitate their faith." Here, the "Word of God" spoken by the prophets of old, spoken by the words of Scripture, and spoken again and anew in the Son of God, *is also spoken by the leaders of the community*. We are thus confronted with the fact of double agency, both human and divine, not only with reference to the Scriptures and, to speak retrospectively, the Incarnation, but no less audaciously with reference to the Spirit-directed proclamation of the Word of God "today." For Hebrews, as later for Karl Barth, there really are three forms of the one Word of God, and Christian proclamation, which surely includes sermonic discourse, must be counted as one of these forms.

The exhortation by Hebrews to imitate the "way of life" and the "faith" of those who proclaim the divine Word should not be taken as an ethos appeal directed to inherently autonomous and competent moral agents as the Enlightenment might insist. As quotations taken from Jeremiah indicate, the ethos appeals in Hebrews speak of those who will be made morally competent *by the Lord* who "says": "The days are surely coming . . . when . . . I will put my laws in their minds and write them on their hearts, and I will be their God, and they shall be my people" (8:8a, 10b; cf. Jer 31:31, 33b). "And the Holy Spirit also testifies to us, for after saying, 'This covenant that I will make with them after those days, says the Lord: I will put my laws in their hearts, and I will write them on their minds," he also adds, "I will remember their sins and their lawless deeds no more"' (10:5–17; cf. Jer 31:33, 34b). The rectitude God requires is the righteousness God alone inscribes.

These re-released transcripts from Jeremiah of the divine Speaker show that Hebrews is saturated with divine promises voiced anew by its human preacher. In a world like this, with daily experiences of torture, imprisonment, degradation, robbery, exile, and execution (10:32–34; 11:32—12:3), God continues to promise his people Sabbath rest where God's will shall reign (4:1). In the meantime to the oppressed faithful, God "has said, 'I will never leave you or forsake you'" (13:5; cf. Deut 31:6). To put it baldly, God literally makes promises to us in the proclamation of his Word, even if these promises are framed metaphorically. This promissory character of God's Word offers a key clue to understanding divine and human agency in preaching and to discovering a homiletic identity for the preacher congruent with it.

Analytic philosophers, beginning with J. L. Austin (1911–1960), recognize that in saying something speakers often perform some act. Promises, such as those in Hebrews, are such "speech acts." More specifically, philosophers classify them as "commissives."[30] Those uttering them commit themselves to doing something either by way of assuming an obligation or declaring an intention. When the Holy Spirit says in Hebrews, "I will remember their sins and lawless deeds no more" (10:17), and when God in that same book promises, "I will never leave you or forsake you" (13:5, cf. Deut 31:6), we have examples of commissive speech. A promise, therefore, always entails its promisor. It always "involves" an agent or subject. In this way, Donald Evans held that linguistic analysis provides a non-supernaturalistic way of accounting for the efficacy of God's Word. When we hear the Christian message with "commissive force," as a promise directed to us, such force necessarily entails the Promisor's self-involvement and simultaneously calls for our correlative response of faith in

---

30. Austin, *How to Do Things with Words*, esp. 150–51 and 162.

the promise.[31] In the words of Christopher Morse, "Faith is present whenever the proclamation of the gospel is heard as God's first-person, present indicative promise to us."[32] No linguistic analysis, of course, can itself reveal that this Agent is in fact God, but linguistic analysis can indicate that there is nothing in the ordinary usage of the language of promise that precludes faith's acknowledgement of the divine Promisor identified as such by the scriptural narrative.

Hebrews testifies that God continues to make promises through their contemporary proclamation by human preachers while using—and subverting—to good effect reigning rhetorical conventions.[33] But nowhere are the human preachers themselves styled by Scripture as "promise makers." While preachers do signify divine promises, they do so in some other name than their own, specifically, in the name of Christ or of the Triune God. Only God can make and fulfill promises, such as the redemption of all creation, that vastly transcend the space and time limitations of the less than Olympian human preacher. And, again, only God can make God's promises credible to faith through the inner illumination of the Holy Spirit. For this reason the Scriptures seemingly prefer the "homiletic tropes" of "witness," "herald," "ambassador," and the like, all of which signal double agency—divine and human— without confusion *and* without separation. Preachers signify the divine promises, but only the divine Promisor can make them significant to the hearers. "Messengers," we are told in

31. Evans, *The Logic of Self-Involvement*, esp. 32 and 164.

32. Morse, *The Logic of Promise in Moltmann's Theology*, 77.

33. A similar pattern is found with Paul, who retains ethos appeals while simultaneously inverting or reversing them in light of his cross-resurrection kerygma. See Resner, *Preacher and Cross*, esp. 105–31.

the Fourth Gospel, are not "greater than the one who sent them" (13:16). That is why preaching depends for its efficacy on the living God, "the one who is speaking" (Heb 12:25–26). For such unpromising types as Abraham and Sarah, and their progeny in our pulpits, parishes, and professorates, nothing less will do.

IV

Promises always entail an outstanding future between their uttering and their fulfillment. As such, divine promises simultaneously proclaim that God has a future, that God is our ultimate future, and that the final shape of the human community "in Christ," "in the Spirit" and "in love" is on its way. Between the uttering and fulfilling of divine promises is the time of grace. For this reason, we can understand the preacher of the gospel as a "messenger of hope" (*apostolos tēs elpidos*). Although you will not find that specific locution in the Bible, it is thoroughly scriptural and congruent with the gospel of God. It is a corollary of the speaking God of the Scriptures whose promissory Word creates, sustains, and empowers communities of hope activated by what the Spirit of God is yet saying to the churches today.

As a messenger of hope, the preacher bears a Word of promise from the living God. That promissory Word may be distilled in a punctiliar cross-resurrection kerygma, summarized in a sentence, or stretched out in a scriptural narrative. In my judgment, it need not necessarily be stated observing the linguistic conventions governing promises, since, metaphorically speaking, the whole scriptural witness to Jesus Christ may be taken as a promise that God wills our salvation. The hearing of promises presupposes both a promisor

and a promisee. Their presence marks interpersonal communication. Uttered promises call for personal response, but
they do not dictate in advance what that response will be. The
rendering of God to faith can never be an automatic property
of the linguistic form of promise, but the linguistic form of
promise is congruent with the rendering of God by God to
faith. While I agree with the Lutheran tradition that preaching and the liturgy, especially absolution, should repeat and
interpret with regularity verbatim scriptural promises, and
that the lack of such in our preaching and worship today is
a sign of our sickness unto death, as a Reformed Christian I
confess that God is free to speak in such a way that human
beings hear the divine promises of salvation even in the absence of their humanly specified linguistic conventions. For
this reason, I would caution against extending the hypostatic
union to embrace a specific form of human language thereby
transposing the Incarnation into "Inverberation." In my judgment, the unique union of human and divine natures in Jesus
Christ should be seen as *analogous* to that coincidence of the
divine Word with human words wrought by the Holy Spirit.
And if this is true, then *ordinarily* we do not have to be shy
about preaching the scriptural promises of God in the form
of linguistically identifiable ones.[34]

34. Here I am responding to the question posed by Lose, in *Confessing Jesus Christ*, whether "in electing the human medium of language, God has made even God's Word to some extent dependent on the human vehicle employed" (165). While divine accommodation to the human linguistic condition pertains to the freedom of God to accompany the creature, that God has elected human language (or bread and wine) does not mean that God is *bound* or subject to these media in the event of revelation.

To hear the proclaimed Word of God as a promise entails God as the promising Subject. This agency, as promissory, is not an impersonal causal mechanism, but personal or existential. God is actively committed to human others in the present and for the future. As a promisor, God includes both a Who and what, that is both self-involvement and commitments that have content. In this regard, while a promise entails a self-involving promisor, it cannot reveal the content of the promisor's character or commitments. For this reason, as postliberalism rightly insists, we need scriptural narrative to identify the God who makes promises. As Richard Lischer has noted, "When the writer of Hebrews declares, 'Faithful is he that promised' (10:23), he is placing that assertion into the context of liturgical observance (10:25) and historical recital (11:1ff.) . . . Thus the promise is not merely *capable* of narration. It *must* be narrated according to the community's memory of salvation."[35] Without such narration, the Triune God of Christian faith would not be "trustworthy." The voice saying, "I will never leave you or forsake you" is not an anonymous caller, but the one identified by Scripture in the events concerning Israel's Messiah.

In my judgment, while the sermon should always witness to God's Word of scriptural promise, the explicit narrative rendering of Jesus Christ in his unsubstitutable identity and particularity is not always required of every sermon, as even Frei's own preaching illustrates. Narrative portrayal goes on in the larger liturgical context of the church, which is also a context of active proclamation and includes the reading of

35. Richard Lischer, "Preaching and the Rhetoric of Promise," 74–75. Lischer argues for "promise as the prototype for preaching" and discusses the rhetorical implications that follow. See 71–79.

Scripture, the singing of hymns, the reciting of creeds, and the services of baptism and the Eucharist. Provided that the story of Israel's Messiah is told and enacted with regularity in the worship of the congregation, the sermon need not carry this responsibility every Sunday. Preaching as promissory narration is best accomplished by a preacher in concert and partnership with the church's life and liturgy.

As messengers of hope, preachers bring tidings not of their own invention. Such promises come from "on high" all the way down to the likes of us, sometimes when we least expect it and when there is no evidence for it. God's Word and promise do not need us to "pump them up" or to make them true. In a world like this, we can only testify and witness to them in the power of the Holy Spirit. As with the Lord's Supper, so in preaching we remember Israel's Messiah, and narrate the covenantal promises renewed in him. Nevertheless, as the Eastern Church steadfastly holds, we also call upon the Holy Spirit, in order that what we remember, identify, and proclaim as saving may be conformed to what is finally true. All sermon preparation therefore must be a prayer for the Holy Spirit to take our offered words, however eloquent or inarticulate, and make them the bread of life. Again, on analogy with the Lord's Supper as "Eucharist," the sermon is an act of worship on the part of the preacher, an oblation of thanksgiving and praise for the faithful God of the promise offered on behalf of the assembled congregation. In this sense, sermons should call forth our best rhetorical efforts and poetic artistry, knowing that all our works are called to give glory to God alone. God's promises in Jesus Christ and in the power of the Spirit enable even preachers to hear anew "the one who is speaking" (Heb 12:25) and in this way boldly to proclaim "the hope set before us" (Heb 6:18).

2

Preacher as Lover

Lucy Lind Hogan

Beloved, let us love one another,
because love is from God;
everyone who loves is born of God
and knows God.
Whoever does not love does not know God,
for God is love.

—1 John 4:7–8

And we are put on earth a little space
That we may learn to bear the beams of love.

—William Blake

All you need is love, love, love is all you need.

—John Lennon and Paul McCartney

BURNING BUSHES or raining frogs might be a better idea. Perhaps, Luke had it right; an evening sky filled with heavenly witnesses singing God's praises and announcing to us all: "Emmanuel"; God is with us and God loves us. These modes of communication would certainly get people's attention and would be much clearer and dramatic.

We declare that we have a communicating God, but a question persists, how does this God communicate with us? How do we come to know who this God is; what God is like? How do we know about our relationship with God and what God would have us do?

The scriptural witnesses to the modes of God's self-communication are, in fact, myriad. God has, indeed, declared God's intentions through burning bushes and raining frogs. God has "spoken" out of a whirlwind, fire, and with a still small voice. Christians proclaim that, ultimately, God spoke as Christ. The Word became flesh and those who knew Jesus knew God. The Word was the word and proclaimed the word.

God has also called and spoken through human messengers. Prophets came proclaiming a startling message: "Thus says the Lord." And for that they were ridiculed, thrown in wells, and threatened with death. Rarely were their announcements welcomed and heeded. (Jonah seems to be the only prophet whose proclamation was received and followed immediately, much to his chagrin.)

The writer of the Letter to the Hebrews reminds us that we *are* surrounded by a great cloud of witnesses. Unfortunately, they are often far from a "heavenly host." Rather, our witnesses are earthly, frail, finite, and all too often, faulty witnesses sent by God to declare the grace-filled message: "Love divine, all loves excelling, joy of heaven, to earth come down."[1]

Human messengers—we have long struggled with this reality. Who are these messengers? We, like Mary ask, "How can this be?" Why would God choose us? Those chosen rec-

1. Charles Wesley, *The Hymnal 1982*, 657.

ognize their feet of clay. They know that they stutter, are too young, or unknown. Moses, aside from questioning his ability as a speaker, knew that the first thing that people would ask him was, "Who sent you? Why should we trust you?"

Consequently, for some, the recognition that human witnesses are untrustworthy has led to the declaration that the only witness to be trusted is the witness of the scriptures. But there are many others who look to and listen to sermon proclamations with that expectation that they will hear a word from the Lord spoken to them in that time and that place.

The modes of God's communication are many; so too are the metaphorical possibilities for describing this preacher. We speak of preachers as heralds, pastors, storytellers, or witnesses.[2] In this essay I will explore one such image rarely utilized, that of lover. However, I would suggest that, as this examination will explain, this should not be thought of solely as a metaphor. Rather, I would suggest that, as Jesus declared, God has called us to love one another. Therefore, to be a Christian is to be a lover; a lover of God and a lover of neighbor. Consequently, preachers *are* lovers—this is not simply a figure of speech.

Our exploration of the preacher cannot begin with a discussion of metaphors or even anthropology, but it must begin with theology. Before we can understand who we are to be as preachers we must first reflect on the God of love who has called us or rather, as philosopher and theologian Jean-Luc Marion observes, "Lets us talk."[3] I will then examine the ways that we understand human love. Then, in turn, I will

2. See, for example, Long's discussion of the images of the preacher in *The Witness of Preaching*.

3. Marion, *God Without Being*, 141.

discuss what it means to be a loving preacher. Along the way we will also look at the ways that we misuse the gift of love.

ENWRAPPED IN LOVE—
BIBLICAL AND THEOLOGICAL FOUNDATIONS

> God is love,
> and those who abide in love abide in God,
> and God abides in them. (1 John 4:16b)

> So I was taught that love is our Lord's meaning . . .
> In this love we have our beginning,
> And all this shall we see in God without end.[4]

Julian of Norwich reminds us that because our God is love, everything that we are and know is enwrapped in love. But, what does it mean to speak of God's love and God as love?

Sallie McFague observes that, "If there is one word the Christian tradition has been willing to apply unqualifiedly to God it is love."[5] Nevertheless, Kevin Vanhoozer, in the introduction to a volume examining theological essays on the love of God notes, "it is exceedingly odd that Christian theologians have . . . been somewhat indifferent—inattentive, neutral—with regard to the concept of the love of God, if we are to judge from their often oblique, indistinct, or awkward treatments of the subject."[6] But, while classical theologians may have been uncertain how to address love—divine and human, Vanhoozer argues that, "A growing number of Christian theologians nevertheless maintain that a major advance in understanding the love of God has been made, a

---

4. Julian of Norwich, *Showings*, 342–43.

5. McFague, *Models of God,* 125.

6. Vanhoozer, *Nothing Greater, Nothing Better*, 1.

step so significant as to entail a paradigm revolution in all of Christian theology."[7] But, before discussing the nature of that revolution, let us step back and look at what the scriptures tell us of the love of God.

His Steadfast Love Endures Forever

In her book, *What We Were Made For: Christian Reflections on Love*, Sondra Wheeler offers a brief but excellent overview of the scriptural witness concerning God's love. Beginning with the Old Testament, she reminds us that, far from the vengeful God of wrath and judgment, the theme of love runs throughout the whole of the Hebrew Scriptures. Ḥesed, is the Hebrew word used for love toward people, especially that love that causes one to recognize that another is in trouble and needs help. It is "the love of God as it reaches from the height of power and holiness to human beings in their weakness and need."[8] Over and over the psalmists and prophets declare God's enduring, persistent love. Ours is a God, they remind us, who is merciful, "slow to anger, and abounding in steadfast love" (Joel 2:13).

The story of the New Testament is the story of God's love made flesh in the person of Jesus Christ, "The love of God, then, is not an idea, nor is it simply a feeling or attitude on God's part. It is an activity, one that leads to the cross. The character of God's love is essentially expressed in this: its readiness to go to any lengths, to the outer limit of self-sacrifice, to restore the relationship that is broken by sin."[9] Gospel

7. Ibid., 2.
8. Wheeler, *What We Were Made For*, 4.
9. Ibid., 11.

narratives and letters tell us of God's nature and activity. And, they call us to be and do love, for we have been made in the image of the loving God.

Over and over again Jesus showed us what love looks like. Love is healing lepers and men born blind. Love is speaking to an outcast woman at the village well. Love is releasing an old friend from the bonds of death. He told us stories about love; about fathers who loved wayward sons, Samaritans who rescued Jews, and shepherds who went off searching for lost sheep. And Jesus called us to love—to love God, love neighbor, love self, and even to love our enemies. If you love me, he reminded us, then we are to care for the least and the lost.[10]

At the center of these scriptural portraits of the God of love is the graceful, overflowing, unearned, unmeritedness of it all. God does not love us because we are so wonderful and beautiful, we are told. God does not love us because we deserve it. No, we are told God loves us because God has chosen to love us in spite of all of our faults and failings, "But God proves his love for us in that while we still were sinners Christ died for us" (Rom 5:8).

A Shifting Paradigm

Christian theology developed between two worlds—Jerusalem and Athens. Out of their Jewish roots, Christians told the stories of the God who created them, loved them, and gave them new life through the death and resurrection of Jesus Christ. They knew that they were God's children, but how were they to understand this loving God and the nature of

10. For a further discussion of the commands to love see Perkins, *Love Commands in the New Testament*.

that love? It was out of their philosophical, Athenian roots that they began to develop answers to those questions.

According to Vanhoozer, classical theology came to describe the love of God as both an attribute and an action.[11] Aware of Plato's concept of love, *eros*, as the desire for something that we "do not have or the desire never to lose what I now have in the future,"[12] Augustine wondered how God could love us. Plato had argued that the gods, who did not need anything, did not love. But clearly the scriptures told us that God does love us. The love of God, according to Augustine was a divine kind of love, *agape*, a gift love.

The attributes and actions of this gift, this divine love, were the focus of theological reflection. According to Aquinas, this love was God willing the good for every person; for the whole world. But, central to this understanding was a portrait of a God who did good for the sake of doing good, but was not moved by that good, "On the traditional view, then, God metes out good but takes neither joy nor delight in the good he brings about (for this would make God's joy conditional on something in the world)."[13] And herein we see the revolutionary shift in contemporary theology.

Rather than focusing on the attribute/action model that pictured God as the immutable sovereign controlling the world, there has been a radical shift toward understanding the love of God as one of relationality. Vanhoozer lifts up the work of a number of twentieth-century theologians. Karl Barth "comes to the conclusion that God essentially is the

11. Vanhoozer, *Nothing Greater, Nothing Better*, 4.

12. Ibid., 4.

13. Ibid., 7.

one who goes out of himself for the sake of another."[14] Jürgen Moltmann argues that we have a suffering God—"we must assert that God, somehow suffers because he loved the world. A God who cannot suffer," Moltmann states, "is poorer than any human ... he is also a loveless being."[15] Our God, they argued is moved by us. How could a distant, aloof, remote God declare to Moses, "'I have observed the misery of my people ... I have heard their cry ... I know their sufferings'" (Exod 3:7). It was this loving, compassionate God who declared, "I have come down to deliver them ... and to bring them up out of that land to a good and broad land" (Exod 3:8).

Vanhoozer argues that for contemporary theologians, to discuss the love of God is to emphasize themes of "sympathy, compassion, mutuality, solidarity, inclusiveness."[16] But he also notes that the paradigm change, in dialogue with the postmodern conversation, is challenging the notion of God's very being. Seeking to move philosophy and theology beyond a metaphysical approach that conceives of God as being, Jean-Luc Marion thinks rather in terms of gift and love. God is the first lover who makes all loves possible. In his introduction to the work of Marion, Robyn Horner observes, "God's first name is love (not being), love is the content of revelation, and revelation is only to be known by loving; this is essentially Marion's complete theological manifesto."[17] We live in the excess, the overflowing of God as love.[18]

14. Ibid., 9.

15. Moltmann as cited by ibid., 10.

16. Ibid., 12.

17. Horner, *Jean Luc Marion*, 66.

18. Vanhoozer, *Nothing Greater, Nothing Better*, 13.

GOD AS LOVER

In her work, *Models of God: Theology for an Ecological, Nuclear Age,* Sallie McFague argues that "traditional imperialistic imagery for God is opposed to life, its continuation and fulfillment."[19] How are we to "interpret Christian faith" for our time and our situation? We live in a world endangered by an ecological crisis; by the threat of nuclear annihilation; and, I would add, global terrorism. Yet, she observes that, "much *deconstruction* of the traditional imagery has taken place, but little *construction*."[20] It was her goal to "remythologize" a relationship between God and the world by developing the models of God as mother, lover, and friend. And of each of these models she asked three questions, "What sort of divine love is suggested by each model? What kind of divine activity is implied by this love? What does each kind of love say about our existence in our world?"[21]

While we may be comfortable thinking of God as our parent or God as our friend, why are we uncomfortable thinking of God as our lover? We may speak of the church as the bride of Christ, yet, as McFague observes, we seem to think that, "Not only should God's love contain no need or interest, it should also contain no desire. It should, in other words, be totally gratuitous, disinterested and passionless."[22] What McFague cannot understand is why this relationship, that is so central to, so important in our lives, why "has this

---

19. McFague, *Models of God,* ix.

20. Ibid., xi.

21. Ibid., 92.

22. Ibid., 126.

model *not* been included centrally in Christianity."[23] To love God, our lover, "We will be united permanently and totally, with the One whom we find most valuable, whom we love beyond all else, and who finds us, the beloved, valuable as well beyond all reckoning. We, begin totally affirmed for who we are, embrace the source of our being and our value: we are 'in love' with the Lover. Our hearts, no longer restless, have found their rest in love itself."[24]

To think of God as lover is to understand the God who is passionately in love with the world and all that dwells therein. This is a God who finds the world valuable and precious. God, the lover, finds separations intolerable and is always at work seeking to heal the breach. Therefore, the activity of God as lover, according to McFague, is saving. Rather than viewing salvation as "a negative event, salvation is holistic, inclusive, and positive . . . God as lover values the world and all its creatures so passionately and totally that God enters into the beloved, becoming one with them."[25] But what's more, to think of God as lover is to think in terms of relationship which means that salvation is not something that is "done" to us. Rather it is something in which we participate as lovers of the God who loves us and who created a world of lovers made in God's image.

Love, Love, Love

It is one thing to speak about the love of God, divine love, the divine gift. But what does it mean to speak about human love?

23. Ibid., 126.
24. Ibid., 128.
25. Ibid., 144.

John Lennon and Paul McCartney reminded us that, "All you need is love." But what does that love look like? How do we live into the love for which we have been created? *"If God's love is the standard, can we hope to meet it?"*[26]

There are many people (not to mention things) I would say I love. I am fortunate that I still have my parents who are approaching ninety. I love my parents in a special way. From them I received the gift of generous, thoughtful love. From them I learned not only what it means to be a parent, but also how to be one who cares for the least. I love my husband whom I have known for forty years. In less than a week we will celebrate our thirty-sixth wedding anniversary. We have had a wonderful journey together, growing and changing. And this journey has certainly had it challenging times as well as moments of great surprise and joy. Together we learned how to be the parents of our two sons whom we love very much. And we now have not only a daughter-in-law, but are excitedly awaiting the birth of a granddaughter, our first.

But that does not even begin to tell you about all of the other people who are very important in my life—sisters, nieces, nephews, friends who are close, if not closer, than family. Jesus called us to love one another. Did that mean that we are to love everyone in the same way with the same intensity? I have to confess, there are some people that I find difficult to like let alone love. Unfortunately, I would agree with Sondra Wheeler's question, can we measure up?

Agapē, philia, eros, storgē; there were multiple Greek words that we often translate with one word, love. Each describes a different human and/or divine relationship. Apologist C. S. Lewis assumed that, when setting out to write

26. Wheeler, *What We Were Made For*, 24. Italics indicate book title.

a book exploring human love, St. John's declaration, "God is love," "would provide me with a very plain highroad through the whole subject. I thought I should be able to say that human loves deserved to be called loves at all in so far as they resembled that Love which is God."[27] Therefore, drawing on the ancients, he first made a distinction between "Gift-love" and "Need-love," echoing the division between *agapē* and *eros* made in the work of the same name by theologian Anders Nygren, *Agape and Eros: A Study of The Christian Idea of Love*.

Lewis quickly realized that the distinctions and descriptions of human love were not so clearly made. Two quickly became four, hence, his book explores the four loves. Affection was what the Greeks called *storgē*.[28] It is the love a parent has for a child. Lewis argued that it is the least discriminating of loves, "warm comfortableness, this satisfaction in being together."[29] It is the humblest of loves.

Friendship, he writes, is the second love. It is the least biological or natural of the loves. It is "essentially between individuals."[30] And while, as he argues, both individuals and community can survive without friendships, he also argues that we, and the community need friendships, "Friendship is unnecessary, like philosophy, like art, like the universe itself (for God did not need to create). It has no survival value; rather it is one of those things which give value to survival.[31]

---

27. Lewis, *The Four Loves*, 11.
28. Ibid., 53.
29. Ibid., 54.
30. Ibid., 88.
31. Ibid., 103.

Eros—to be in love, is the third love. This love, romantic, sexual, "is really and truly like Love Himself. In it there is a really nearness to God."[32] But he would also admit that, in this love, in eros, we can find great pain and sorrow. As McFague observes, "in a love relationship, betrayal and estrangement can turn feelings of attraction into feelings of anger; great love engenders strong emotions at both extremes."[33]

Finally, Lewis describes charity. In contradistinction to the first three loves, which he identifies as the "natural" loves, natural "Gift-loves," charity is the "Divine Gift-love." This divine gift enables us to love "what is not naturally lovable; lepers, criminals, enemies, . . . the sulky, the superior and the sneering."[34] This love is not in our nature. Rather, it comes by grace which opens our hearts and minds to the other. This is the grace that allows me to love even those I do not like, "they are receiving Charity, are loved not because they are lovable but because Love Himself is in those who love him."[35] With this grace we come to love the Lover, the One whose love is overflowing. This, Lewis describes as "Appreciative love." This is the grace, the gift that "lies at the true centre of all human and angelic life. With this all things are possible."[36]

---

32. Ibid., 153.

33. McFague, *Models of God,* 132.

34. Lewis, *The Four Loves*, 177.

35. Ibid., 183.

36. Ibid., 191–92.

Love Misplaced

While Lewis may have viewed love as a gift of grace, Sondra Wheeler reminds us that we also have to learn how to love thoughtfully, carefully, respectfully. To love, she argues involves our will, our judgment, our care for the other, but also our passions and feelings.[37] There is a discipline of love as well as a gift. For we often find too many cases where love is misplaced and abused. This is a crucial dimension of love as we move into thinking about preachers as lovers. There are clearly boundaries within which we must remain if we are to explore this image of the preacher.

Sallie McFague opines that we have avoided speaking of God as lover because, to do so, is to raise the issues of eroticism and sexuality. And, unfortunately, it is not too difficult to find cases of clergy who have taken this image seriously and literally. As I was working on this essay one such case came to light.

A Roman Catholic priest in Miami was a very popular pastor as well as media star. Thousands flocked to his church. Millions more visited his website, read his books, and watched his appearances on Oprah. In fact, he came to be called "Father Oprah." The focus of his ministry was to help people explore issues of relationships, sexuality, and morality in a contemporary, nonjudgmental way. The title of a recent book was, *Real Life, Real Love*. As he explained in a newspaper interview, "Rather than fighting this reality, you want to inspire people on a personal level to live the best way they can.

37. Wheeler, *What We Were Made For,* 101.

... I constantly tell people that the church is not a museum for saints but a hospital for sinners."[38]

Unfortunately for Father Cutié, when photographs of his passionate embrace of a bikini clad woman on a Florida beach were plastered all over the newspapers, he found that his bishop was actually expecting more "saintly" behavior on the part of one of his priests. He was relieved of his parish duties. "Father Cutié made a promise of celibacy and all priests are expected to fulfill that promise with the help of God," declared his bishop, Archbishop John C. Favalora. "His actions cannot be condoned despite the good works he has done as a priest."[39]

I would hope that, as we explore this image for preachers we would heed Luther's admonition, *abusus non tollit usum,* "abuse does not destroy the use." The image of preacher as lover brings a depth that we do not always find in other images and metaphors. At the same time, the recognition that the pastoral relationships have at times been abused should serve as a cautionary warning but not denial of this richness.

A STILL MORE EXCELLENT WAY— SPIRITUAL GIFTS FROM THE GIFT

But God, who is rich in mercy,
out of the great love with which he loved us
even when we were dead through our trespasses,
made us alive together with Christ—
by grace you have been saved. (Eph 2:4)

38. Boorstein, "Our Father Who Art in Flagrante," sec. C, p. 4.
39. Ibid., 4.

One who experienced that overflowing love was Paul, the one "untimely born" (1 Cor 15:8). He recognized that, "I am the least of the apostles, unfit to be called an apostle because I persecuted the church" (1 Cor 15:9). Nevertheless, "By the grace of God I am what I am, and his grace toward me has not been in vain . . . so we proclaim and so you have come to believe" (1 Cor 15:10a, 11b). Paul was fully aware of his faults and foibles. He knew that he was an unlikely and unbelievable messenger of God. Like Moses, he knew that people would be hesitant to trust him and would ask, "Who sent you?" Paul knew that that grace and love that made his conversion and ministry possible were gifts of the one who is that gift.

In his letter to the nascent church in Corinth, Paul helped the new Christians explore the gifts that God had given them in order to build up the Body of Christ. He knew that this gift from the one who is the Gift was not something to be kept and horded. Paul recognized that, while different people had been given different gifts, each person and each contribution was necessary for the growing of God's reign.

Paul reminds them of the various "parts" and functions of the body. The contributions of prophets, teachers, and healers were to be essential to the growth of the Body of Christ. Yet, while we focus so much on Paul's description of these gifts, we miss an important transition that follows this message. While encouraging people, not only to recognize the gifts they have been given, but also to "strive for greater gifts" (1 Cor 12:31a), Paul points to perhaps the greatest of all gifts, "I will show you a still more excellent way" (1 Cor 12:31b). And that way is love.

Noisy Gongs and Clanging Cymbals

Tradition gives us a number of portraits of preachers as lovers. Paul observed that, without love, we would be "noisy gongs" and clanging cymbals" (1 Cor 13:1). In the *Phaedrus*, Plato, in the guise of Socrates explores the nature of rhetoric and the character of the speaker with his student, Phaedrus. Phaedrus had just heard a speech by Lysias about the nature of speakers. Lysias had argued that it was better that a speaker be a non-lover, who could control his feelings, than a lover who is "afflicted" with the disease of passion. Socrates rises up to make a contrary speech in which he describes the non-lover and the false lover. Ultimately, however, he wants to argue that the speaker must be the true lover, "Thus the desire of the true lovers, and the initiation into the mysteries of love, which they teach, if they accomplish what they desire . . . is beautiful and brings happiness from the inspired lover to the loved one."[40]

As Peter stood on the beach with the risen Christ he was confronted with the challenging question, "Do you love me?" (John 21:16). All that he was to do, all that he was to be was to be grounded in this fundamental relationship of love; God's love for him and his love of God. To live into the reign of God, we are to love God, and to love our neighbor. The call to serve God is not only a call to proclaim this good news, but it is also a call to enter into relationships of intimacy and risk. We have been loved into being by the God who gave all for us on the cross. And we, in turn, are asked to give all that we are and all that we have for the other.

40. Plato, "Phaedrus," 493. This has been, in turn, considered by Richard Weaver in his essay "The *Phaedrus* and the Nature of Rhetoric," 3–26.

Noisy Gong—The Non-lover

While we might wish to promote the preacher as "non-lover" or the one who steps out from the preaching relationship in order to facilitate a direct relationship between God and the listener, we do this at some peril.

Lacking love for the other, Griffin describes the non-lover as "the legalistic lover."[41] This person, he argues, ignores Christ's command to meet the "human needs for food, peace, dignity," choosing instead to persuade solely out of a "sense of obligation or duty" and is "only going through the motions."[42]

The non-lover, according to Weaver, in an effort to be practical and detached offers speech that is objective, "mind to mind," and universal. "We have compared its detachment with the kind of abstraction to be found in scientific notation."[43]

Is it possible to be detached and uninvolved? I would argue that, whenever we speak, our listeners are making judgments, not only about the content of our discourse, but about us as well. Can they trust us? Do we know what we are talking about? Do we care about them? Therefore, to approach the preaching moment from the stance of the non-lover, or the one who seeks to stay out of the message, thinking that it is only God who is speaking, is not only impossible, but naïve.

Clanging Cymbal—The False Lover

The exchange between Peter and the risen Christ would indicate that the relationship of love between humans and

41. Griffin, *Mind Changers*, 39.

42. Ibid.

43. Weaver, *Phaedrus*, 9.

between the human and divine can be open to question. The question must, therefore be, not only "do you love me," but also "how do you love me?" Scripture and experience tell us that there are those who approach the other with malevolent motives and false ends. For the preacher who is a false lover, the listener is one to be manipulated and possessed. This lover is, as Socrates observes, an exploiter not a defender or advocate.

Richard Weaver labels this "base rhetoric," whose end is exploitation, "influences us in the direction of what is evil."[44] And the base rhetorician is one who "is not motivated by benevolence toward the beloved, but by selfish appetite,"[45] viewing the listener as property rather than an independent equal.[46] Em Griffin provides us with an extensive taxonomy of false lovers, e.g., the flirt, the seducer, before he arrives at our final portrait, the true, noble lover.[47]

The Greatest of These—The Noble Lover

God has shown us this more excellent way. God has been, and continues to be the true and noble lover who is "the way and the truth and the life" (John 14:6). The preacher who is a noble lover honors and respects the other. The true lover is willing to risk all for the other. In his description of the true lover, Griffin observes that this is the preacher who "cares more about the welfare of the other ... [and] respects the hu-

---

44. Ibid., 11.
45. Ibid., 10.
46. Ibid., 13.
47. Griffin, *Mind Changers*, 32–39.

man rights of other people."[48] Or, as Weaver argues, this is the person who is in "a generous state which confers blessings to the ignoring of the self."[49]

The noble lover, described by Paul, is the preacher who is patient, kind, "is not envious or boastful or arrogant or rude. This lover does not insist on her/his own way; is not irritable or resentful; does not rejoice in wrongdoing, but rejoices in the truth" (1 Cor 13:4–7). The preacher who loves the other, "bears all things, believes all things, hopes all things, endures all things" (1 Cor 13:7).

PREACHER AS LOVER

What does it mean to challenge preachers to ground their preaching in a relationship of love? What would be the characteristics of the loving preacher?

To be a preacher is to respond to the call by the one who loved us first and gave himself for us. It is to learn love from the one who is love. As Marion reminds us, God overflows with love and we, in turn are to overflow with love for the others. Or, as Evelyn Underhill described it, we are to have the, "humble and genial devotedness as we find in the most loving of the saints. I mean the quality which makes contagious Christians; makes people *catch* the love of God from you. Because they ought not to be able to help doing this, if you really have got it: if you yourselves feel the love, joy, peace, the utter delightfulness."[50]

---

48. Ibid., 40.
49. Weaver, *Phaedrus,* 13.
50. Underhill, *An Anthology of the Love of God,* 220.

The preacher who is a lover is someone who is passionate and excited about the call to share the good news. This is not someone who is detached or unemotional. Love is about caring for the other and worrying about what happens to the church and the world.

As Sallie McFague reminded us, a lover is one who is concerned about bringing a saving, healing word. The lover preacher searches out places of brokenness and pain, and is willing to suffer with those who are suffering.

The loving preacher is one who respects and values the other. To be a lover is to care about and shape a message for the listener. As John McClure observes in his description of "other-wise preaching," it is "a form of preaching that is constantly interrupted by the proximity of the other, by an obligation to the other, and by what Levinas calls the 'glory of the Infinite' given in the face of the other."[51]

Loving preachers recognize that each listener is different and they enjoy and honor those differences. They love the others for who they are and do not expect them to change in order to suit him or herself. Rather, we are all to grow into the fullness of our life in Christ. The loving preacher looks beneath the surface to the heart, the depth. As Joseph Jeter and Ronald Allen observe, "In the same way that the ocean contains many different kinds of fish, the typical congregation contains many different kinds of people who are defined by many different traits. [Therefore] preaching calls for variety that corresponds to the variegation in the listening community."[52]

---

51. McClure, *Other-wise Preaching*, 9.

52. Jeter and Allen, *One Gospel, Many Ears*, 5–6; see also Nieman and Rogers, *Preaching to Every Pew*.

In the end I return to Sondra Wheeler's question, is this possible; can we measure up to the call that we have been given? As one who has preached for almost thirty years, I will testify to the fact that I have failed more times than I would care to admit. I have not been always been patient or kind; rather, I have been irritable and resentful. But I will also testify that God, the gracious lover, has taken my message with its finite, inadequate words and turned them into glorious proclamations of the good news. With God, all things are possible, and it is through the grace of God that women and men with feet of clay, foibles, and faults are able to become truly loving preachers declaring, "Thus saith the Lord."

3

Preacher as God's Mystery Steward

Preaching Healing in an Apocalyptic Frame

André Resner

Recently, I received an email from a student. His brother was diagnosed with pancreatic cancer this past fall and died within a month. He told me that he had gone to Detroit to be with him and to pray for his healing. He prayed with boldness and confidence, fully expecting God to cure his brother. After the funeral he returned home only to have a church member be diagnosed with the same disease. She appeared to take a turn toward recovery after everyone began praying, yet within two months she died too. He confided in me that his faith had hit the rocks. He is a Christian minister and his flock and his family look to him for strength and words of hope, but he has none right now and after watching an episode of Oprah where a medical doctor was doing depression screenings, he suspects that he may now also be clinically depressed.

It is natural to struggle with illness, loss and grief. But, unwittingly, preachers have often compounded problems associated with these all too real experiences by their simplistic approach to the cure stories in the gospels. I am increasingly impatient with the way preachers uncritically "apply" the gospel cure stories, setting people up for disappointment, anger, guilt and worse—wholesale rejection of God, Jesus, Christianity and church.[1] The question remains, however, what are we preachers to do with the healing stories in the gospels? After all, they have a dominant presence in the gospels and come up regularly for preachers who follow the lectionary. One path through the difficulty is to see the preacher's task as a kind of word management of God's mysterious ways of working. Hence, a newly retrieved image for the preacher, God's mystery steward.

DIFFERENTIATING PREACHING THE BIBLE AND PREACHING THE GOSPEL

An important differentiation is critical at the outset of a discussion of how to preach from the healing stories of the gospels. Preachers need to remember that just because the Bible narrates something does not mean that what is narrated is what preachers should preach or attempt to "apply." If that were the case, watch out when we get to the story of the bald-headed (and rather sensitive) prophet Elisha, the boisterous boys and the mauling she-bears (2 Kgs 2:23–24). If

1. One can see an example of this type rejection in Neil Young's song, "Soldier," from 1970. Young muses about Jesus' eyes and how they have a certain allure. In the end however, Young concludes, "Jesus, I don't believe you, because you can't deliver right away."

one believes that whatever the narrative gives us is to be simplistically "applied," the preacher might admonish the youth
to be very careful how they speak to follicle-ly challenged
ministers or God might kill them too. A preacher whose theological sensitivities guide his or her reading of the narrative
for preaching the gospel can't help but see a dramatic abuse
of prophetic power in the story, a misuse that might function
in a sermon dealing with contemporary misuses of ministerial power.[2] And how can a preacher whose understanding
of God and the gospel from the larger landscape of theology,
scripture and experience read the story of Jephthah's bad vow,
and subsequent murder of his daughter in the name of Godly
"radical obedience" (as I heard it preached once), and not
with a "gospel-conscience" preach against the narrative since
it so violates that larger view of God and the gospel (Judg
11:29–40)?! As much as God wishes us to take our vows seriously (Ecclesiastes 5), I believe God wishes us to take the lives
of our children even more seriously. Repent of the bad vow,
Jephthah!

Those two examples are dramatic, of course. Yet, the
extreme narratives in the Bible, while not the real problem
since they are rarely if ever used in preaching, nevertheless
help us see the underlying hermeneutical problem inherent
in all preaching that attempts to use biblical texts. For once
we ask a gospel oriented question of those texts, like, "Are the
actions of Elisha here consistent with what we know about
God and how God wants prophets and ministers to use divine power and authority?" we see more clearly the problems
and the possibilities inherent in how we might make a move

2. Cf. the unpublished sermon by Scott Black Johnston, "In the Name
of the Lord," preached in Plainfield, New Jersey in 1991.

to application in a sermon that is in conversation with those texts. For unless we make the Elisha story the canon for our understanding of how God wants prophets to use prophetic power, we see that his use of that power is in great contrast to what we know about God from the larger prophetic canon, and what we know about God's expectations for how prophetic and ministerial power is to be exercised.

So, ironically, the biblical texts that pose the most problems for preachers are not the extreme texts, but rather the stories with which we are all very familiar, perhaps too familiar. Once we recognize that a gospel orientation to reading and using biblical texts for preaching is the appropriate hermeneutical strategy in preaching, what is exposed is our un-gospel and even anti-gospel use of texts that we have too easily assumed were homiletical cakewalks. Yet it is this uncritical use and application of texts that creates the greatest theological and psychological fallout for preachers and their hearers. For very often preachers do not bring the same hermeneutical discretion, i.e., a perspective from the vantage point of a "working gospel," to the familiar texts that we bring to extreme texts, like the Elisha and Jephthah stories. It becomes clear when we come to the problem texts from the vantage point of a working understanding of the gospel that they prove problematic for preaching, especially when we ask how those narratives might be applied or how those narratives "speak to us today." What preachers need to do is bring that same discretion—a gospel sensitivity—to every text that they encounter. Not to do so is to functionally assume a fundamentalist position, one that is becoming manifest in homiletical theory through what Abraham Kuruvilla identifies as a "pericopal theology" in his *Text to Practice*.[3]

On the other hand, in *Preaching the Bible and Preaching the Gospel*, Edward Farley argued that preachers must remember they are not called to preach the Bible per se, but rather the gospel. An understanding of the gospel guides our reading and use of any biblical text in preaching. Moreover, the Bible's agenda in any given set of verses may not sync with preaching's agenda. Neither was the Bible written to give preachers in twenty-first century North America 6–12 verse sermon segments, each with a guaranteed "preachable X" inside the confines of each hermetically sealed sermon nugget.[4] Recognizing this, the question becomes: how do we preach the gospel in conversation with the healing stories of the New Testament in ways that do not compromise the gospel itself? That statement, however, leads to another question: What is the gospel?

3. Kuruvilla presented the idea of pericopal theology as a way of understanding preaching as a bridge between the ancient text and contemporary proclamation in a paper, "The World in Front of the Text: An Intermediary Between Text and Praxis," at the 2008 annual meeting of the Society of Biblical Literature. His argument in the paper and the book illustrates my point here. His pericopal theology assumes that every sermon-sized nugget of the Bible contains in equal measure the gospel. Therefore, preachers do not need to have a working understanding of the gospel that they bring to each text, since every text, simply by virtue of being in the Bible, is the gospel. My argument is that preachers who are not clear about their working gospel and how it functions in their reading of texts for preaching *de facto* practice pericopal theology.

4. Farley, "Preaching," in *Practicing Gospel*, 77–78. Poll any group of preaching students on how long a passage of scripture should be for preaching. The interesting consensus is 6–12 verses. How does anyone know that before even knowing what text is being considered?

The definition of the gospel is, I believe, the most assumed aspect of Christian preaching. Yet, there is little consensus at present in homiletical theory or in preaching practice on how gospel is to be defined.[5] One's working understanding of the gospel guides the way one reads and interprets scripture and how one interprets and incorporates into preaching all other factors—e.g., one's self, one's cultural and congregational situation, and what one believes God to be doing in our world. "Working gospel" is to apply an insight from David Tracy.[6] With reference to the idea of the "canon within a canon," he argued that the concept of a "working canon" was a better way of understanding how the Bible actually functions for people as they try to think "biblically," since no one can have the whole Bible operating at once in their consciousness and it is highly unlikely that anyone would have a fixed set of texts exclusively functioning for them in the sense that the phrase "canon within the canon" implies. "Working gospel" suggests the sense that we have a way of understanding what God has done, is doing and will do, but it is not necessarily fixed to any one set of content. Some have argued for certain specific sets of content to be definitive for the gospel, such as the death,

5. Sample the work especially of David Buttrick, Edward Farley, Ronald Allen, and Paul Scott Wilson. The more theologically consistent a particular preacher is, the more discernible the "working gospel" of that preacher. Barbara Brown Taylor is a good example of someone whose "working gospel" permeates almost all her sermons, regardless of the biblical text she is in conversation with. One might argue that this would constitute the sin of *eisegesis*. That charge hinges on an uncritical assumption about the homiletical efficacy of historical criticism, which, when carried over into homiletics, results in "pericopal theology," the assumption that every pericope regardless of location or length contains what ought to be preached, i.e., the gospel. Cf. note 4.

6. Tracy, *The Analogical Imagination*, 254 and 290 n. 28 and n. 29.

burial and resurrection of Jesus (1 Cor 15:1ff.). But each concrete manifestation of God's redemptive activity is another instantiation of gospel. I argue that the death and resurrection of Jesus can be seen as the pinnacle event of God's redemptive, gospel, activity in the world, but it is not the only such instance of God's gospel-ling actions.[7] That particular event might be seen as the pivot event toward which all former and subsequent acts of God point and radiate.

My working definition of the gospel is not a temporal description of some one act of God, but is rather hermeneutical: *the gospel is something that God does that human beings cannot do for themselves, that concretely changes a situation from . . . to. . . .* Let us examine briefly each element of this definition.

First, *the gospel is something that God does that human beings cannot do for themselves.* Much preaching, as Paul Scott Wilson has pointed out, leaves God out and moves to human action and morality.[8] Yet, from the gospel's perspective, all human action is responsive and derivative of God's prior action. "We love because [God] first loved us" (1 John 4:19). This aspect of the definition asks, *"What in the world is God doing?"* The preacher looks for concrete ways that God continues to manifest God's redemptive activities in the world. These ways are discernible using a certain kind of "*discrimen*," or lens of

---

7. The Apostle Paul's understanding of gospel is broader than one piece of static content as can be seen in Galatians 3:8, "And the scripture, foreseeing that God would justify the Gentiles by faith, declared the gospel beforehand to Abraham, saying, 'All the Gentiles shall be blessed in you.'"

8. Wilson, *The Four Pages of the Sermon,* passim, but see 37–44 in particular.

discernment that, like a literal lens, has been "ground" to allow for a particular kind of sight.[9]

Second, *the gospel concretely changes a situation from ... to ...* The gospel, the heart of which is God's action, cannot consist of only abstract assertions. Rather it must narrate the lived experience of our encounter with God's transforming actions, in the biblical texts and in our world. Wilson has called this the "deep structure" of the gospel.[10] I find the metaphor of "grammar" in reference to the gospel useful in understanding the structural nature of what we proclaim. The "*from ... to ...*" part of my definition attempts to identify a key element of the gospel's grammar: God's actions address, undress and redress some specific aspect of the human situation. The "*from*" identifies a place in our Reality that is in a state of compromise from what God desires to be. The "*to*" identifies where and how God's actions redemptively change the situation. The "to" points toward the Vision.[11] The gospel is firstly that God *addresses* our Reality, exposes our failures and idolatries—or whatever stands in opposition to what God wants and wills to be in this world. The gospel is secondly that God *undresses* our Reality, revealing the layers and structures of sin and disobedience that lie in, under and throughout particular actions and situations. The gospel is thirdly that God *redresses* our Reality. God does not leave it as it was but

9. "*Discrimen*" is the term David Kelsey uses for the pre-understanding that is necessary to understanding any new situation; Kelsey, *The Uses of Scripture in Recent Theology*, 160–69; cf. Hilkert, *Naming Grace*, 93–96.

10. Wilson, *Four Pages*, 25–27.

11. Stephen Johnson, *Apocalyptic Eschatology as Homiletical Deep Structure,* uses the language of "over against" and "toward." He calls these the bifocal, deep structural elements of the Gospel's inherently apocalyptic nature.

brings about some redemptive, cleansing and rejuvenated movement toward God's Kingdom ways and Vision for how things ought to be. The gospel consists of the ways that God fills the gaps between our Reality and God's Vision for how things ought to be. Gospel ministry is that which participates with God's work in-between a fallen Reality and an initiated and impending Vision. Preaching gospel gives voice to this spectrum and identifies concrete ways that God sweeps us up into the same kinds of redemptive actions. The church's mission takes its cues from the way that it identifies the gaps between Reality and Vision and the way it participates in concrete means of joining God's work of filling the gaps. Arguably anything that does not participate in these concrete instances of "gap-filling" is a waste of the church's time. By extension, any preaching that does not participate in this ministry of gap-filling is a waste of words.[12]

One further step is necessary in filling out the job description of God's mystery steward. Any preaching of the gospel must attend to the gospel's inherent apocalyptic framing, as the Apostle Paul was at pains to do. If it doesn't, then it is very easy for preachers to effectively collapse the gospel's inherent apocalyptic frame and preach "healing = cure now," a kind of preaching that violates both the apocalyptic nature of the biblical texts and the gospel proclamation. Such preaching charts a problematic theological course for hearers and sets them up for disappointment with God by creating ill-founded expectations for how God acts.

In order to more clearly understand how apocalyptic frames our gospel preaching, the image of the preacher as

12. Cf. Resner, "Social Justice," 135–37; cf. also Campbell's *The Word before the Powers*.

God's mystery steward helps orient preachers to a more theologically appropriate sense of identity and function, especially in the use of the gospel cure stories in preaching.

PREACHER AS GOD'S MYSTERY STEWARD: ATTENDING TO THE APOCALYPTIC FRAME

As I said earlier, the image of the preacher as God's mystery steward is not new. I am retrieving the image from the Apostle Paul, because although Paul considered it the key for reorienting the Corinthian Christians to a rightful understanding of just who its community orators were and were not, the tradition since Paul has largely ignored the image.[13] Paul forged the image of the preacher as apocalyptic steward of God's mysteries on the anvil of the Corinthian church's cultural, social and theological misunderstanding of their community orators and leaders. We will examine: 1) the Corinthian church's perceptual problem; 2) how Paul intended the image of the preacher as God's mystery steward to help reframe their consciousness; 3) how the image might help us imagine the preacher's work today; 4) with specific application to reading the gospel healing stories for preaching.

The Situation in Corinth

The Corinthian Christians carried baggage from their sociocultural situation which distorted their perception of themselves and their community orators/leaders, i.e., preachers.

13. A search on www.Amazon.com will show a number of books and sermons that use the image in their title, but I have not found any development of the image in books or sermons consistent with Paul's apocalyptic emphasis.

Drenched in first-century Greco-Roman culture, their baptism had not washed away the way they esteemed the speech-maker-preachers in their midst. Community orators were philosophers of significant status from whom they too could gain status. They were their time's Rock Stars and celebrities. The Corinthian Christians had a problem with Paul because though he was one of their community orators, he was becoming more and more of an embarrassment to them for breaking all the decorum rules of their world, a world shaped by the suppositions of classical rhetoric.[14] Paul's list of social humiliations was long, but consider just the matter of patronage. For Paul, taking money for ministry, a common practice in his day for someone with means to support an itinerate philosopher, would put him in a potentially compromised relationship of dependency on a wealthy person who might then have certain expectations of Paul. To refuse patronage was to break friendship and would insult the patron. Paul was damned if he did and damned if he didn't. From the vantage point of the cross-event-proclaimed however, Paul chose the damnation that was closest to his gospel. He chose the risk of alienation by humiliation (menial labor and poorer living conditions) because it more closely embodied the humiliation of Christ. Climbing the social ladder of patronage would have been more in conflict with the grammar of his gospel since it would have meant exaltation and even possible advancement and greater prestige. For Paul's argument in 1 Corinthians to make any sense to his readers, they would have to abandon their old ways of perceiving speaker/hearer

14. Cf. Peterson, *Eloquence and the Proclamation of the Gospel in Corinth*, 66–69. See also Lucian, *On Salaried Posts in Great Houses,* vol. 3, 411–81.

relationships and take on new ways of knowing and perceiving, ways derived from their participation in Paul's apocalyptic message and the community life that derived from that message.[15] Paul's reframe of the person of the preacher by way of God's apocalyptic working in the cross and resurrection is thoroughly humiliating for both preachers and congregation. And, naturally, people do not welcome humiliation. Paul is at pains to argue that, for those in Christ, preachers are to be seen (i.e., their *ēthos*) not as high status philosophers but as servants and slaves (*diakonoi* and *hypēretas*). Their message (*logos*) was not wisdom and heavenly sign but foolishness and scandal. And they, the Corinthian Christians, how are they to view themselves (*pathos*)? "Consider your own call . . . not many of you were wise by human standards, not many of you were powerful, not many of you were of noble birth. But God chose what is foolish . . . what is weak . . . what is low and despised in the world, things that are not" (1 Cor 1:26–28). His reframe was not pretty and it was "in their face," i.e. confrontational. He humiliates his readers as no prize when God called them. They were the low hanging fruit that God picked to be his very own. Paul's message and method resembles very little of the self-esteem pep rallies of many churches in North American contexts. In order to change their perceptions of preachers from Rock Stars to slaves, Paul deploys a new and subversive image: God's mystery steward.

There are three parts to the image. First, the preacher is "steward" (*oikonomos*). An official position in households that could afford such workers, the steward was usually a high

15. Cf. Brown, *The Cross and Human Transformation;* Resner, *Preacher and Cross*; Gorman, *Cruciformity*; and Knowles, *We Preach not Ourselves.*

ranking slave who was entrusted with managing most if not all of the matters pertaining to the owner's household.[16] The closest thing in our culture now may be the personal assistant. The two key facets to this position are: 1) stewards are not owners of the things with which they are charged; and 2) stewards must prove trustworthy and will be held accountable for how they manage the owner's things.

Second, the owner in the case of preaching is God, and it is to God that preachers of God's message are ultimately accountable. In contrast, according to the rules of classical rhetoric, the audience was king and decided who did well and who did poorly, who persuaded and who was implausible. This difference is not a small matter, and is the key to the whole problem Paul faced with the Corinthian Christians. To think like a rhetorician meant beginning with the audience and gauging everything with them in mind. To think like a preacher of the gospel meant beginning with God and gauging everything with the gospel's purposes in mind. The gospel is meant to be heard, of course, but the hearer does not determine for the preacher what will be said nor how it will be said. In a manner which would have befuddled his recipients (and many contemporary preachers and homileticians) Paul argued that the rhetorical situation of Christian proclamation is one in which preachers are accountable not to those who hear but to God who is the owner of the preacher's message.[17]

16. Reumann, "'Servants of God,'" 339–49; Reumann, "*Oikonomia*," 147–67.

17. Not only that, but Paul argued that even personal judgments about one's self must be kept in check because all temporal judgments of God's preachers are shrouded in ambiguity. It will be "the Lord . . . who will bring to light the things now hidden in darkness and will disclose the purposes of the heart" (1 Cor 4:5). In our day and time Paul's

Such a fact calls into question all attempts to determine the "effectiveness" of preaching by measuring the results of how hearers feel about what they hear, unless—and this is a big unless—those hearers are using epistemic criteria for the gospel which are consistent with God's apocalyptic gospel. In that case, hearer-feedback can be trusted rather than questioned as self-serving.[18]

Third, the "things" that the steward of God manages are God's *mysteries*. What are the *mysteria*?[19] Paul's audience in Corinth would again have had plenty of cultural baggage attached to the word "mysteries" because of the prevalence of mystery religions all around them. In using the term Paul risks misunderstanding, but for Paul the risk is worthwhile in light of the potential gain. If he can accomplish the epistemological reframe of the church's consciousness, they will be able to interpret all from their past and all in their present according to their new apocalyptic categories.

In the context of Paul's 1 Corinthian letter, *mysterion* is closely related to the word of the cross, Christ crucified proclaimed (1 Cor 1:23; 2:1, 7). In Paul's argument, the preaching of the gospel is itself the revelation (*apocalypse*) of the mys-

---

words should function to make humble and careful all human boards, bishops or other bars of judgment before whom ministers stand to be authorized for ministry. At the same time Paul's words cannot be used by unscrupulous people to justify acting apart from denominational means of discernment.

18. Current discussions in homiletical theory keep arguing around the access of the appropriate starting point. Cf. Hogan and Reid, *Connecting with the Congregation* with Kay, *Preaching and Theology*.

19. Cf. Tripolitis, *Religions of the Hellenistic-Roman Age*; Martin, *Hellenistic Religions;* and Meyer, ed., *The Ancient Mysteries: A Sourcebook*.

tery (1 Cor 2:7, 10). That does not mean that we control God's revelation by our preaching or thwart God's revelation if we do not preach. The revelation of the mystery is itself mysterious. As Bornkamm explains, God's revealed mystery is always attended by hiddenness.

> Since the *mysterion* of God as such is disclosed in revelation, its concealment is always manifest with its proclamation. The antithesis implied in the *mysterion* is 1. the antithesis between the then and the now . . . 2. the constant antithesis between the rulers of the world and those who love God . . . , and, 3. the antithesis between the now and the one day . . . hence the revealed mystery still conceals the final consummation. The eschatological enactment is still only in word, the fulfillment of all things is as yet only through the church, *doxa* (glory) is only in the concealment of *thlipseis* [tribulation/ suffering].[20]

What the world sees as one thing, the church sees as another. What the world hears as one thing, the church hears as another. What the world experiences as death the church experiences as life. The cross embodies the difference. To the world it is a functional expletive, a form of torture and death reserved for the most despicable and notorious. To the church, the cross becomes the sign of life and hope and even resurrection and eternal life. It also serves as the lens of critical discernment for the church over against the world's ways of knowing and valuing. It is thus a critical symbol of ongoing discernment. It functions as a means of hermeneutical suspi-

---

20. Bornkamm, "*Mysterion*," 822.

cion on the deceptive ways the world tries to sell people lies and temporal, yet deadly, happinesses and hopes.

Paul mentions "mysteries," i.e., in the plural, in 1 Cor 4:1.[21] Paul knows that the ways of God—God's mysteries— are ways that are ultimately beyond the processes of human knowing, and, at the same time, those ways are revealed in concrete acts—what God has done, is doing and will do. God's ways are deeds of revelation that are, again by God's mysterious will, connected to the proclamation of those mysteries. Proclamation as revelation evokes faith and awe, resistance and rebellion, community and mission even as it prompts a sense of understanding and participation in God's secret and salvific ways, or further blinding and unbelief. God's mysteries are given in such a way that they can never be owned, completely captured or confined to a particular form or content. And yet, those mysteries show a consistent dynamic: 1) a temporal, finite and fragile content, and, 2) a sub-structure that owes to apocalyptic, especially as a broad, sub-structural, way of understanding the nature of time and God's use of it.

Paul's gospel was framed by an apocalyptic consciousness. No dispensable Kantian husk around the gospel, to remove the apocalyptic frame would be to change the gospel into something else. The apocalyptic consciousness is generated by the real life gaps between the Vision for the way God actively wills the world to be and the way the world really is in its fall-

---

21. He much prefers the singular and only uses the plural here and later in 1 Cor 13:2 and 14:2. The former seems to be a reference to the many secret things that might possibly be known, the latter to ecstatic utterance of *glossalalia*. The use in 4:1 suggests that Paul means more here than he does by the use of the singular in 2:1 and 2:7.

en state—Reality.[22] Scripture bears witness to God's ongoing ways of willing and acting to bring about God's redemptive and whole Vision over against the fallen and resistant Reality. From the first day of creation to the "Day" of consummation, everything in creation groans toward fulfillment, adoption, redemption, toward the full fruits of the kingdom of God to be manifest and for light to extinguish darkness once and for all. Preaching the gospel participates in this and is itself a kind of *crying* out to God, a *groaning* toward the redemption of all creation, and a *sighing* of visceral participation in the Spirit's pleading with the God who has promised an ultimate resolution to history's conundrums.[23]

The act of God in Christ, especially in the climactic event of the crucifixion and resurrection, is God's *penultimate* instantiation of Divine intervention and the closing of the greatest of gaps and fissures in both the seen and unseen realms of existence. It is penultimate in the literal sense of the term, "last but one." It signals that something has begun that is yet to be finished. Penultimate means that there will be a finish, that this act requires another. The act of God in Christ on the cross and in the resurrection of Jesus from the dead represents the first fruits of the fulfillment of God's as-yet-to-be-fulfilled Vision. Nevertheless, in the death and resurrection of Christ God has decisively opened a new, healing and

22. Beker, *Paul the Apostle.*

23. Romans 8 describes the work of the Spirit in those who struggle in the wait for adoption and full redemption. The primary role of the Spirit is described there as helping give voice to those who suffer in the in between time, voice in crying, groaning and sighing, all communications to the Promiser about the desire for fulfillment, and all function to help the sufferer not lose hope but to latch more securely onto the promise. I will take up Romans 8 and develop it more later in this chapter.

anticipatory future for the world, one that will be completed at the *parousia*. That event represents the turning of the ages from old and toward new, with the defeated powers of darkness and destruction continuing to exert themselves onto the present from the age of death.[24] At the same time, the age that is yet to come sends beams of light and hope streaking across the darkness. The now represents a time of conflict, tension, revelation and concealment.

J. Paul Sampley has schematized this apocalyptic moment in a manner that depicts the grammatical sub-structure of the gospel (see figure 1—Apocalyptic Frame of Promise-Fulfillment). The disclosure of God's redemptive actions in face of the bad news casts a look forward into the realm of the new age where God's ultimate resolution and triumph lies.[25]

24. Martyn, "Epistemology at the Turn of the Ages," 264. In the experience of his son's death, Nicholas Wolterstorff put his finger on practical aspects of the apocalyptic gospel working its agonizing way in faith's struggle. Someone remarked to Wolterstorff, "Remember, he's in good hands." Wolterstorff's response illustrates the now but not yet character of our faith in God's actions in Christ: "If I had forgotten about the resurrection then that reminder would have been . . . but I did not see death as a bottomless pit . . . nevertheless . . . death still stalks this world and one day knifed down my Eric," Wolterstorff, *Lament for a Son*, 31.

25. Sampley, *Walking Between the Times*, 108–9.

Fig. 1: Apocalyptic Framing of Promise/Fulfillment

Sampley's schema shows the grammatical sub-structure of the gospel. The disclosure of God's redemptive actions in face of the bad news casts a look forward into the realm of the new age where God's ultimate resolution and triumph lies. In the meantime we see partial, though only temporal, fulfillment with hope for fullness. That partial fulfillment gives meaning, and in some cases a kind of temporary healing, even if permanent cure is as yet still anticipated.[26]

---

26. Black, *A Healing Homiletic*, 51. In discussing the strategy of plotting the arc of celebration in preaching, Frank Thomas is careful to note how celebration can function apocalyptically in the experience of the sermon: "*Celebration is the culmination of the sermonic design, where a moment is created in which the remembrance of a redemptive past and/or the conviction of a liberated future transforms the events immediately experienced*"(italics original); Thomas, *They Like to Never Quit Praisin' God*, 31. Farley, in his early attempt at defining what for him is an ultimately un-definable gospel writes, "To proclaim means to bring to bear a certain past event on the present in such a way as to open up the future," Farley, "Preaching the Bible and Preaching the Gospel," 80.

PREACHING THE GOSPEL IN CONVERSATION
WITH THE CURE STORIES IN THE GOSPELS

Let me now extend this one step further into one difficult locus of preaching, namely preaching in conversation with the healing stories of the gospels. Kathy Black has helpfully pinpointed a key issue in using these particular texts in preaching: "How we preach the biblical narratives that deal with persons who are blind or deaf or have leprosy can be healing or oppressive for persons with those disabilities today."[27] Black makes a helpful differentiation between *healing* and *cure*. Often, when preachers preach on narratives that tell about a character who is cured, they unwittingly extend the claim for cure simplistically into the present.[28] When cure does not happen, theological gymnastics are performed: the uncured person didn't have enough faith, or, the uncured person is being punished by God for sin, or, tested by God, or, being taught a lesson, or, we can't quite tell at the moment but we have to be confident that God is working out some blessing by means of the continued illness or disability. The preacher always has an out by blaming the person who is already suffering.[29] Thus, this kind of preaching compounds the pain of those who are already in pain and renders to them a distorted

27. Black, "A Perspective of the Disabled," 6.

28. Cf. Black, *A Healing Homiletic*, 19–42.

29. Romans 8:28 is often deployed just here ("We know that all things work together for good for those who love God, who are called according to his purpose") as a simplistic solution to the gap the sufferer is experiencing. Ironically, the verses preceding v. 28 hold the key to the sufferer understanding the gap and how v. 28 is a word of assurance that makes sense only out of an experience of suffering, crying, groaning and sighing in the power of the Spirit.

God who *can* cure people (just look in the Bible story), but doesn't choose to cure them right now. If questioned, the preacher can always blame some faith-defect or hidden sin in the sufferer. Job's friends are alive and well. Black argues that the preacher's problem is not that of helping people determine whether God is malevolent or benevolent in face of their suffering. She asserts that God is benevolent, not finicky: "we are confident that God wills our well-being."[30]

Indeed, the picture we see of Jesus bringing wholeness and cure in the gospels is testimony to the fact that God indeed wills wholeness and well-being for all human beings. Just how preachers are to understand how God wills that today, or any day that falls between the time depicted in the gospels and the time of Jesus' *parousia*, and how God uses healing power in our time, is where things often break down.

Misuses of the healing stories in preaching stem from a failure to see those narratives within the framework of their apocalyptic substructure. Using the gospels in preaching the gospel requires that preachers preach their "kingdom of God" nature. The person of Jesus to whom the gospels bear witness was the embodiment of the fullness of God's highly anticipated reign. In these narratives we see, in some specific and sporadic incidents, what the reign of God will look like in the day of fulfillment. In the presence of anything less than complete wholeness, we witness dramatic eclipses of the fragmented and broken with health and wholeness. Everyone in Jesus' path, and thus everyone in the path of God's reign, is cured and made completely whole, for the time being.

The gospels thus give us a glimpse into an apocalyptic and eschatological perspective. A state announced and in-

30. Ibid., 21.

stantiated in Jesus' person, but one which, in those gospel narratives, we only see the first fruits of, and, now anxiously long for along with a groaning, eager to be delivered, creation (Rom 8:22–23). What we see in Jesus' person and his encounters with all manner of persons is what will be when the highly anticipated kingdom of God becomes fully present. But in using these texts in preaching now, God's mystery steward needs to be very clear to point out some important differences between the circumstances borne witness to in the text and our circumstances. The most important difference is that *Jesus is not with us here and now the way that he was back there and then*. If he were, we could expect cure (albeit, temporary) wherever he set foot, hand, eye, spit, or, wherever he sent word and, thus, "authority." But his foot, hand, eye, spit and word are not with us in the here and now the way that they were then. Nor are those aspects of his being with us now the way they will be, we anticipate by hope, in the promised future. Therefore, we now find ourselves in that tensive time, the in-between-time, where we anticipate eternal wholeness, but cannot unequivocally expect even temporary healing in the present time. Sometimes someone may experience a healing that is not a cure, sometimes a healing that resembles cure, but in the here and now it is *always a healing that is temporary, not permanent*. Jesus is the only character to have gotten out of the New Testament alive. Everyone else eventually died. Lazarus had two funerals, as did the little girl to whom Jesus said "*Talitha cumi*." The unfortunate prerequisite for resurrection is death.

As Kathy Black helps us see, God and our faith can bring healing to our lives—"a sense of well-being in the midst of disability. Faith helps people live with their disabilities."[31] Faith also helps us live toward the horizon of God's coming reign. That lean toward God's future is experienced now as a yearning for the fuller, eschatological wholeness when we believe God will ultimately deliver all flesh and all creation in God's ultimate victorious future.

Plotting this dynamic on the schematic that Sampley proposed clarifies the tensive quality of the preacher's proclamation of the impending eclipse of the old age and the present time by the promised future. Our current time is one in which the realities of the coming age are proleptically present, thereby transforming the lives of those who embrace this good news from despair to hope, from fear into confident faith. In addition, the mission of the church is sparked to further enflesh in the present time the realities of the coming age, thus God's people are empowered to lives that express justice and love and stand over against injustice and hate, since these have been dethroned, disempowered and their ultimate end has been signaled. The reality of the impending future changes the potentiality of the present (see fig. 2—the Apocalyptic Frame of Fragmented/Whole).

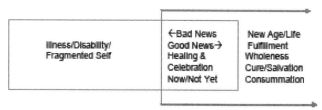

Fig. 2: Apocalyptic Framing of Fragmented/Whole Self

31. Black, "A Perspective," 23.

Preaching that fails to take into account the under-girding grammatical substructure of apocalyptic collapses the hoped-for future into the present. The result of the collapse is a relaxing of the tension in the now with a resultant distortion of the gospel, sometimes called realized eschatology or over-realized eschatology. The homiletical fall-out of this collapse is significant. For the gospel is distorted into health, wealth and prosperity "gospels." For Paul in Corinth, it was the heretical "gospels" of triumphalism and enthusiasm that he countered with his word of the cross in its apocalyptically tense form. For North American Christians it is now the gospel of prosperity ("God wants to bless you with material prosperity") and health ("healing = cure, now!") that must be countered with a cruciform message under-girded with a sturdy apocalyptic sub-structure. When the future is collapsed onto the present, the anticipated new age is simplistically used to trump and effectively eclipse the now with its ongoing struggles. Premature celebration becomes a kind of denial of present suffering rather than anticipatory prayer.[32] All present suffering must be addressed by the preacher with a hybrid language that co-mingles gospel words of ultimate triumph along with the language of lament and longing in order to maintain truth and balance. The distorted gospel of "prosperity and/or cure

32. As indicated in n. 27, Frank Thomas is careful in his description of the role of celebration not to have preachers collapse the future pole into the present. Yet when the preacher moves into the celebration movement of the sermon, the age to come can be anticipated in the preacher's and congregants' joyful expression. Indeed, the preacher's move of celebration, according to Thomas, evokes contagious hope in God's promised future. Celebration that is "caught" by the hearers acts as a "ecstatic reinforcement" which works on both cognitive and emotive logic, thus driving home assurance and true change; Thomas, *They Like to Never Quit Praisin' God*, 84–106.

now" must include an element that deals with the failure to deliver. It thus works itself out in all the attempts to explain why, even though the preacher proclaims health and cure and prosperity, it doesn't happen for everyone: "You must not have enough faith." "You must be being punished for some sin." "You must be being tested." "God must be teaching you something." All of these are convenient excuses for a failed homiletical paradigm. More disastrously, preachers who do not steward God's apocalyptic gospel pin God's failed actions to cure now on those who are already suffering, thus compounding their pain. I cannot imagine a more fraudulent manner of speech, one more ethically compromised, than that which exchanges the apocalyptic gospel for one that sells fabricated hope and eventually results in producing in the hearers either guilt or despair and frustration and ultimately leads to those sufferers giving up on God and faith. Preaching as stewarding God's mysteries refuses to collapse the promised, future, triumph of God into fantasy, present-day experience where all gets made better, right now, if we just believe enough and if we just "name it and claim it." The present time, rather, is characterized by struggle and trouble, by the bad news of our fallen experience for which God has worked out, is working out and will work out a good news conclusion. In such a time we sometimes get temporary glimpses of God's coming glory and conclusion, but not ultimate, permanent, fulfillment. See Fig. 3, Apocalyptic Frame-Blindness/Sight, for more images as plotted on the Sampley schematic.

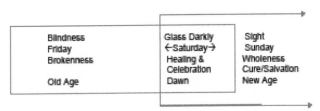

Fig. 3: Apocalyptic Framing of Blindness/Sight

Helping people live in the often paradoxical, ironic, and tension-filled dynamics of the in-between-time is perhaps the greatest need for preaching in our present time. Preaching which prematurely resolves the inherently irresolvable pre-*parousia* issues of human existence and suffering compounds human suffering and destroys people's hope and faith.

For Paul, the present age is one of eager longing for the completion of our adoption. In the absence of the physical presence of Jesus as we see him portrayed in the gospels, the church has been given the gift of the Holy Spirit. And the Holy Spirit's chief role among believers in this present age is to help us not give up faith or hope in God's ultimate triumph. Romans 8 describes three tangible ways the Spirit sustains believers. The Spirit helps us 1) to cry out to God, 2) to groan as with labor pains (along with creation) as we wait for our full adoption and redemption of our bodies, and 3) to trust our exasperated sighs to be the Spirit filling in the blanks of prayers that we do not even know how to pray. Paul's apocalyptic understanding of time and hope from Romans 8 is schematized in Fig. 4, a third possible expansion of Sampley's schematic.

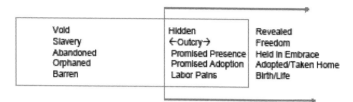

Void	Hidden	Revealed
Slavery	←Outcry→	Freedom
Abandoned	Promised Presence	Held in Embrace
Orphaned	Promised Adoption	Adopted/Taken Home
Barren	Labor Pains	Birth/Life

Fig. 4: Apocalyptic Framing of Slavery/Freedom

Preaching the gospel is an exercise in apocalyptic testimony. The things God has done, is doing and will do are inexhaustible mysteries, yet by God's grace they have been disclosed in such a way that we can discern not only particular instances and actions but also a sub-structural grammatical plot. Part of what it means to be faithful to what we have been entrusted to preach means being faithful to the apocalyptic schema, i.e., taking care to situate every sermon we preach within the apocalyptic frame. Doing so will prevent our preaching from becoming triumphalistic, from setting up people's hopes such that they cannot be fulfilled. People abused by non-apocalyptically framed preaching are left to feel angry or guilty but not enriched or buoyed by God's ultimate and anticipated triumph. That triumph is only partially seen, heard and experienced now. Faith and hope anticipate God's impending fulfillment in face of God's mysterious delay.

The gospel narratives of cure are localized and temporal witnesses to the work that God wills to do to bring about the fulfillment of God's Vision for creation over against the Reality of decay and death. Preaching the apocalyptic gospel of hope and healing consists in using those narratives to show what

God ultimately wills, and will ultimately bring about. Faithful use of these stories, though, also maintains the tension that these narratives create. They bear witness to something that anyone who suffers wants: cure, healing, wholeness, what appears to be the complete eradication of suffering. Closer examination reveals their temporal character, however. They are witnesses in the sense that they point toward something much greater than the temporary cure in the situation. They point toward a permanent cure for all creation that is on the horizon. As reminders, they renew and sustain hope in God's initiated, though incomplete, acts of redemption. They also remind us not to shrink our world to the size of our particular suffering, a problem that all suffering of any kind threatens to do. They help create solidarity among all sufferers who yearn for healing, fulfillment and justice. Yet it's important to remember in the pre-parousia world, even when we mysteriously experience fulfilling instances of healing we are to recognize, that each such instance is only a temporary shadow of what God will bring about in the end. Thanksgiving, praise and celebration is appropriate at such times, as is the continued prayer, often in the form of lament, for ultimate fulfillment.

Sickness, suffering and death are aberrations on God's good creation. They are not part of what God wishes or wills for humankind. They are truly bad news realities for which God desires eradication in the form of some kind of *sotēria*, salvation, wholeness. Thus, Jesus' ministry of cure that we see so powerfully in the gospel narratives gives us a true glimpse into what God does will for humankind's pain and suffering and even death. God wills life and wholeness. They are a window into the unseen world that we now embrace by faith. They force a reconsideration of the seeming finality of what we experience in the world—aging, decay, illness, and ultimately death. But it's important to note what the gospels tell us and what they do not tell us. A quick and easy movement from what we see in the gospels to what God is doing today misses the most critical element in those narratives: the person of Jesus and his incarnated presence. That presence was localized in his body and limited to wherever his body went or wherever he sent word, and thus power. Villages not on his itinerary did not receive that power and cure. People one street over from his path remained in whatever state of brokenness they were. Tax collectors who climbed trees on the wrong street did not have *sotēria* come to their house that day. The gospels make it clear that when people became aware that Jesus was in the vicinity, everyone scrambled to gather up all their sick and demon-possessed friends and relatives and bring them to Jesus. This was their chance and since he was on the move, they might not have another tomorrow.[33]

So we see two amazing things in these narratives: 1) in Jesus' person, in his bodily presence, the Kingdom of God is fully present; and 2) wherever God's Kingdom of shalom is fully present no brokenness, no disability, no illness of body, mind or spirit will go untouched or un-cured.[34]

33. Only keeping the Sabbath, since breaking it carried a possible death penalty, was more important to the people than getting their sick and demon-possessed friends and relatives to Jesus (Mark 1:32–34).

34. Space does not permit the necessary next step of reading and interpreting specific texts with a view to preaching the gospel. A subsequent work by the author will develop this project in precisely that direction.

CONCLUSION

This essay began with a problem that many of us know well: the experience of the loss of a loved one to an illness in spite of prayers to God for healing and cure. Expectations for healing by prayer have been fueled by preachers who have uncritically and simplistically "applied" the cure stories in the gospels with promises of the same kind of cure for people today.

I have argued that these experiences of loss in spite of prayer to God are not failures of the faith of those who pray or the failure of a God who is either malevolent or impotent. Rather, these losses are to be seen in the theological framework of apocalyptic. Plotted beneath the grand drama of human history, the gospel bears witness to the ways that God has not abandoned God's creation but has instead definitively addressed creation's fallen state, and in the death and resurrection of Jesus Christ, has spun history into a new direction, away from death and toward life, away from brokenness and toward wholeness, away from slavery and toward freedom, away from sin and toward salvation, away from despair and toward hope. Our present time is one in which we find ourselves between the times, that of Jesus' first coming and his second. The gospels of the New Testament grant us a window into what the world looks like when God is fully present, and they give us hope and strengthen our faith so that we can be sustained during the time between the times of God's full presence. The Holy Spirit resides with us now as we wait. And that Spirit helps us hang on, especially through pain, loss and grief, primarily through the means of articulation of longing: cries, groans and sighs. Good homiletical stewardship of this drama helps people to see what God has done, is doing and will do, thus enabling those who suffer to renew and deepen faith while they live in the in-between time. Thus the image that clarifies identity: Preacher as God's Mystery Steward.

Faithful stewardship of the gospel in preaching means plotting our sermons, especially those that are in conversation with the cure stories of the gospels, on the framework of apocalyptic. It means not succumbing to the temporary temptations to promise more than we've been given in the present, namely, pre-parousia cures. It means not naming the bad news of our time as temporary sickness or poverty, for which the message of preaching becomes a newly packaged health and wealth gospel of healing and prosperity. Such approaches to preaching have proven to build the fame and fortune of a few preachers, but they have not proven to create and sustain a people of faith who join in God's contemporary struggle against evil and injustice. The apocalyptically framed gospel closes the backdoor of the church, where unfulfilled and disappointed sufferers limp out feeling anger, guilt and wondering whether they can muster any kind of faith in God anymore.

The image of the preacher as God's mystery steward helps reorient contemporary proclaimers of the gospel to their mission and to the trust that God has given them. It reminds them whose ministry and message this is, namely, God's. It helps free preachers from any culture's temptation to reduce Christian ministry and the gospel message to mere optimism or wishful thinking. It resituates preachers' imagination to take in the long view and to help them read the biblical texts with a view to how the gospel helps them see how these texts might function in preaching. The image helps remind preachers that they are stewards, not owners of the word of the gospel. And as stewards, they are accountable to God for the expectations they create in people and the hope to which they point people. It is easy in North American culture to abuse our trust and to turn the gospel into a commodity, one that can raise wrong hopes at the same them that it feeds the preacher's ego and personal pocketbook. As God's mystery stewards, preachers are reminded that their job is not to resolve everyone's problems but rather to open up mysteries—God's revealed and hidden mysteries—so that people can live within their mystery and power and be drawn in faith toward the promised horizon of God's coming kingdom, no matter what suffering, loss or grief they face. Living in the power and promise of God's mysteries, we can, like the Apostle Paul, come to realize that even when prayers for healing go unfulfilled in the present that God's grace is nevertheless sufficient for us (2 Cor 12:9).

4

Preacher as Ridiculous Person

Naked Street Preaching and Homiletical Foolishness

CHARLES L. CAMPBELL

FOR SOME time now, I have been interested in alternative forms of preaching—practices of preaching that take place outside the traditional pulpit and sanctuary. These forms of proclamation rarely make it into the preaching textbooks or the serious homiletical literature or even the histories of preaching. Nevertheless, although usually overlooked in homiletics, these forms of preaching, I suspect, have some important things to teach us.

Over the past few years, I have particularly been interested in street preaching, which is what I call a form of "extreme homiletics." Street preaching is a tradition that is much richer and more diverse and often more grace-filled than our contemporary stereotypes of it would suggest. And street preaching is much more widely practiced than some of us might think. Even though it gets relegated to the backwaters of homiletics, every tradition—from Evangelicals to Presbyterians to Methodists to Roman Catholics to the Salvation Army—has affirmed and engaged in this practice in one form or another.[1]

Recently I have discovered an even more extreme form of preaching. It is a subset of street preaching—the most extreme form of preaching I have yet encountered. And that would be *naked* street preaching. I'm not joking, and I'm not speaking metaphorically. This is real. And when I first came across this particular practice of preaching, I thought, Wow! This might be a sufficiently obscure topic for academic research.

As I began to do some research, however, I discovered that naked street preaching is not quite as esoteric as I first imagined. There is actually a much more extensive literature about the naked street preachers than I thought there would be. Now, I have found nothing about them in the *homiletical* literature. And I haven't found anyone who calls them "naked street preachers"—the term is somewhat anachronistic. However, these figures are regularly discussed in the literature about holy fools. In addition, some traditions, particularly the Orthodox tradition, and especially Russian Orthodoxy, have actually valued naked street preaching. In these traditions naked street preachers are not simply odd, historical curiosities, but actually at times venerated saints of the church.

For example, consider the famous St. Basil's Cathedral on Red Square in Moscow—the cathedral with the glorious onion domes and fanciful colors. Many of you have seen it in photographs, and I suspect some of you have even visited it. Well, that cathedral is named for St. Basil, the Blessed, who

1. See Saunders and Campbell, "Street Preaching," in *The Word on the Street*, 95–107.

has been called "the naked prophet of the streets."[2] For over *seventy* years in the fifteenth and sixteenth centuries Basil wandered the streets of Moscow year round—often stark naked—enacting, proclaiming, and embodying the gospel for the people of the city. (One of his miracles, someone has noted, was simply surviving so many Russian winters.)[3] Basil called sinners to conversion. He prophesied future events. He performed strange sign-acts, such as throwing rocks at the homes of those who made a public display of their alms-giving and kneeling to kiss the pavement before "houses of ill-repute." He engaged in extraordinary ministries of kindness toward the poor. And ultimately he invited people into the presence of Christ. On August 2, 1588, this naked street preacher was officially made a saint in the Russian Orthodox Church.

While Basil may be the most famous naked street preacher, there are many others. The heyday, as best I can tell at this point, seems to have been in sixteenth-century Moscow. Basil was clearly not the only naked street preacher of his day. As one foreign traveler to the city during that time reported, there are "certain hermits . . . who go stark naked [and are given] liberty to speak what they list without any controlment."[4] And some of these naked street preachers have names. There is Vasilii of Moscow—called "the one who goes around naked."[5] And there is Andrei of Constantinople, who received instructions in a dream, "Be

---

2. Forest, *Praying with Icons,* 138.

3. Ibid.

4. Murav, *Holy Foolishness,* 19.

5. Ibid., 24.

naked and mad for my sake."[6] There were also a number of women, such as St. Mary of Egypt, who embraced nakedness as a form of devotion, though they tended to be ascetics in the desert, rather than public figures in the cities.

Naked street preaching, however, is not simply confined to the East. In the West, for example, St. Francis of Assisi engaged in it. At a critical turning point in his ministry, Francis stripped naked before the Bishop in the public square of Assisi, proclaiming his freedom *from* his father and his freedom *for* God. Standing naked in the square, he cried out: "Listen, listen, everyone. From now on I can say with complete freedom, 'Our Father who art in heaven. Pietro Bernardone is no longer my father, and I am giving him back not only his money, . . . but all my clothes as well . . . I shall go naked to meet the Lord."[7] It was one of the most provocative acts of testimony in his ministry.

Then, of course, there's the Bible. As my former colleague, Walter Brueggemann, would say, "don't blame me; it's in the text." The great patron saint of naked street preaching is the prophet Isaiah himself, as we read in Isaiah 20:

> In the year that the commander-in-chief, who was sent by King Sargon of Assyria, came to Ashdod and fought against it and took it—at that time the LORD had spoken to Isaiah, son of Amoz, saying, "Go, and loose the sackcloth from your loins and take your sandals off your feet," and he had done so, walking naked and barefoot. Then the LORD

6. Ibid., 27

7. Green, *God's Fool: The Life and Times of Francis of Assisi*, 82–83. Francis is also reported to have climbed into a pulpit naked in order to preach on the nakedness and humiliation of Christ. See Wright, "Fools for Christ," 27.

said, "Just as my servant Isaiah has walked naked and barefoot for three years as a sign and a portent against Egypt and Ethiopia, so shall the king of Assyria lead away the Egyptians as captives and the Ethiopians as exiles, both the young and the old, naked and barefoot, with buttocks uncovered, to the shame of Egypt. And they shall be dismayed and confounded because of Ethiopia their hope and of Egypt their boast. In that day the inhabitants of this coastland will say, 'See, this is what has happened to those in whom we hoped and to whom we fled for help and deliverance from the king of Assyria! And we, how shall we escape?'"

And at the very heart of the gospel is Jesus' act of naked street preaching. He was stripped, hung beside the road on the cross, and mocked by the passersby—the Word made flesh. And while many of us often don't pay much attention to the shame and vulnerability of Jesus' nakedness on the cross, others throughout history have highlighted this dimension of Jesus' death. In the second century, for example, Melito of Sardis wrote in his *Homily on the Passion*,

> He who hung the earth [in its place] hangs there, he who fixed the heavens is fixed there, he who made all things fast is made fast upon the tree, the Master has been insulted, God has been murdered ...O strange murder, strange crime! The Master has been treated in unseemly fashion, his body naked, and not even deemed worthy of a covering that [his nakedness] might not be seen. Therefore the lights [of heaven] turned away, and the day darkened, that it might hide him who was stripped upon the cross.[8]

8. Hengel, *Crucifixion*, 21.

In his own way, Melito of Sardis captures what Paul calls the foolishness and weakness of the cross.

This foolishness and weakness, embodied in the shame of nakedness, shaped the ministry and witness of the naked street preachers. They sought to enact in extreme ways the foolishness of the cross proclaimed by Paul in 1 Corinthians 1:18–25. Like Paul himself, they became "fools for the sake of Christ" (1 Cor 4:10). For the naked street preachers, the character of the preacher actually merges into their message as the preacher's life itself becomes a sign-act that proclaims the gospel (similar to Isaiah and other prophets, whose lives often became one with their message; and similar to Jesus, whose life was one with his Word). They enact the Word, rather than simply announcing it verbally. The extreme practices of the holy fools, as someone has summarized, "may be seen as a pale imitation of the . . . message of the cross."[9]

The naked street preachers, in fact, remind me a bit of the characters in Flannery O'Connor's short stories. Many of you know those characters—they are often bizarre, even repulsive. When O'Connor, a Christian author, was asked why she wrote such strange stories with such grotesque characters, she replied, When you're writing for those who are "almost-blind, you draw large and startling figures."[10] To put that another way, "When you're preaching for people whose imaginations have grown numb, you may have to preach with large and startling figures." And the naked street preachers did just that: they sought to embody the foolishness of the gospel in big and shocking ways. In fact, they frequently appeared on the

9. Murav, *Holy Foolishness*, 96.

10. O'Connor, *Mystery and Manners*, 34.

scene when the church was becoming complacent—numb—and needed to be startled back to its calling.[11]

As you might imagine, faced with such bizarre figures, theologians have interpreted the naked street preachers—the holy fools—in a variety of ways. Medical science and psychology have also weighed in on these characters, but I'll have to leave those interpretations for another time.

One typical theological interpretation views holy fools as dramatic examples of faithfulness and virtue. A sermon I recently discovered on the internet provides a good example of this widespread approach.[12] The sermon takes as its starting point the life and ministry of the naked street preacher, Basil, the Blessed. Yes, I actually found a fine contemporary sermon dealing with Basil, the Blessed on the internet. You just never know! Following a brief presentation on Basil's life and ministry, the sermon makes three clear, carefully ordered points about the importance of the holy fools for us today. First, the preacher states, "Fools for Christ are calling us to make the love of God supreme in our lives." Second, fools for Christ call us to care far less about pleasing the world and far more about pleasing God." Finally, "the fools for Christ teach us that humility is the way of salvation." And the sermon concludes, "The beauty of humility shines brightly from the Fools for Christ, and is calling us to imitate these sacred jesters." Here naked street preachers are depicted primarily as examples of faithfulness and virtue. They become odd and extreme embodiments of a kind of *personal ethic*. The preacher abstracts

11. Saward, *Perfect Fools,* 215.

12. Trenham, "Fools for Christ"; online: http://www.saintandrew .net/fr_josiah/homilies/fools_for_christ_pnt8.htm.

virtues from the lives of the holy fools and holds these virtues up for all of us to emulate.

I don't want to deny the truth of these insights. This preacher undoubtedly captures important dimensions of the fools for Christ. However, I don't think this approach gets to the point. It doesn't take seriously enough the holy fools'—and particularly the naked street preachers'—extreme, bizarre, and even obscene behavior. I'm not convinced that these figures are best understood primarily as embodiments of more abstract virtues like love and humility, which we are called to emulate. Consider, for example, Symeon the Fool of sixth-century Syria. He first entered a monastery and then became a hermit living in solitude. In both of these ways he embodied the virtues of faithfulness and humility in an extreme form. Then, one day, Symeon walked into a city in Syria dragging behind him the carcass of a dead dog that he had gotten from a dung heap outside the town. And the next day he went to worship and tried to extinguish the candles in the church by throwing nuts at them. And then he took to eating enormous quantities of beans, which had the desired effect. (Please, no comments on sermons you've heard.) There's something else going on here—something more than the virtues of love and humility. Folks like Symeon and Basil were, as one scholar has noted, deviants outside *both* the structures of society *and* the conventions for fleeing that society.[13] Indeed, other scholars have argued that the holy fools should in fact *not* be understood primarily as examples to be imitated. Their ministry was a specific charism that was not meant for everyone, but

13. Krueger, *Symeon the Holy Fool*, 2.

served a specific function within their particular context.[14] So, I think we need to go a bit deeper.

And the last line of the sermon I just discussed actually points us to a deeper place. The naked street preachers were in a very real sense, as the preacher concludes, "sacred jesters." As some have argued, these holy fools engaged in an intentional, carefully orchestrated kind of street theater. They offered up a kind of daily "carnival" that unmasked the social hierarchies and decorum of the day and turned the wisdom and power of the world on its head. They lampooned and burlesqued social structures and systems shaped by the power of sin and death in order both to unmask human sin and to help set people free from the powers.

In a general sense, their nakedness, if you will excuse the pun, exposed the realities of a world in which clothing was quite concretely a sign of social hierarchy and status and security. In a dramatic way, through their "big pictures," they lampooned an entire system, which was often embodied in different kinds of clothing. They rejected the seduction of that system and enacted their freedom from it. And they invited the people of their time to a similar freedom from that system's hierarchies and securities.[15]

In addition to this general challenge to the powers of the world, the naked street preachers often engaged in more focused political acts—acts not unlike those of the jester. St. Basil, the Blessed, for example, became a kind of "court jester"

14. Saward, *Perfect Fools*, 214–15.

15. Forest, *Praying with Icons,* 142. One of the places this hierarchy of clothing plays itself out in particularly striking "fashion" is at the convocations, graduations, and inaugurations that take place at institutions of higher education. The term "regalia" (as in "academic regalia") is related to "royalty," even "sovereignty."

to Tsar Ivan the Terrible, speaking truth to power and challenging the brutalities of Ivan's reign. On one occasion during Lent, Basil presented the Tsar with a huge slab of beef. When Ivan replied that he didn't eat meat during Lent, Basil responded, "Why abstain from meat when you murder so many [people]."[16] Ivan was apparently so troubled by Basil's constant challenges that he lived in dread of Basil and would allow no harm to be done to him. And the Tsar even attended Basil's funeral.

Isaiah engaged in a similar kind of unmasking during his three years of naked street preaching. In his particular context, he dramatically exposed the foolishness of relying on military and political alliances—particularly alliances with Egypt—in the face of the Assyrian Empire.[17] More broadly, however, I think Isaiah was exposing the consequences of a world ruled by the domination and violence of Empire or superpower. In such a world, innocent civilians become victims who are oppressed and shamed. Isaiah made that crystal clear.

The truth of the prophet's naked street preaching is not limited to his day. Consider a photograph from June 8, 1972. I'm sure most of you have seen it. It is the photograph of a nine-year-old Vietnamese girl running naked down a street, her arms outstretched in the form of a cross, a cry of agony on her face. Three-fourths of her body has been burned by napalm, and the smoke of her flaming village rises in the background. That photograph became an icon during the Vietnam war, a contemporary embodiment of Isaiah's prophetic sign act. It

16. Ibid., 138. This legend about Basil is told in several different versions and is also attributed to another holy fool, Nicholas of Pskov.

17. Brueggemann, *Isaiah 1–39*, 168.

exposed in a graphic and shocking way the consequences of a world ruled by the domination and violence of superpowers. Like the naked street preachers, that photograph held before us in a dramatic way Paul's affirmations about power and weakness, wisdom and foolishness. And in the Iraq war similar forms of domination and violence have been exposed in the photographs of naked prisoners taken at Abu Ghraib prison.

And on the cross—in Jesus' act of naked street preaching—a similar kind of unmasking occurs. Through the weakness and foolishness of the cross, Jesus brings the powers of domination and violence out into the open. He exposes them for what they are—not the powers of life, as they claim to be, but in fact the powers of death. On the cross, as we read in Colossians, Jesus disarmed the principalities and powers and made a public example of them, triumphing over them (Col 2:15).

This understanding of the cross represents one of the most extraordinary contributions of the naked street preachers. They understood that the cross was not just about personal forgiveness or individual justification, but also about the public unmasking of the powers of death that seek to rule the world. So they embodied the foolishness and weakness of the cross in the public square, making a public example of the systems and powers that seduce us and hold us captive and prevent us from living into the full freedom of the gospel. They enacted the truth in that old Christus Victor model of the atonement, according to which Jesus tricked the devil, drew him out into the open, made a public example of him, and triumphed over him.

I confess, I like this interpretation of naked street preaching. From this perspective, the holy fools become an embodiment of a *social ethic* that fits nicely with the interpretation of preaching I have developed in recent years. In fact, this understanding of the naked street preachers initially stirred my interest in them. Ah, I thought, a dramatic, if bizarre, confirmation of my own homiletical ethic! The Word before the Powers. It was perfect!—the naked street preachers fitting neatly into my own homiletical framework—manageable and understandable.

But then I read another book. And the naked street preachers turned on me in a troubling way. They began to unmask and lampoon the foolishness of homiletics itself—the foolishness of both preaching and teaching preaching. The book is *Holy Foolishness: Dostoevsky's Novels and the Poetics of Cultural Critique*, by Harriet Murav. In the book, Murav recognizes the dimensions of naked street preaching I have already mentioned. But she takes their work to a deeper and more troubling place.

Murav refuses to abstract either a clear *personal ethic* or a dramatic *social ethic* from the lives of the holy fools. She refuses to distill some virtues for our personal lives or a process of resistance for social engagement. She focuses instead on the bizarre particularity and concreteness of the naked street preachers' witness. In this scandalous particularity, she argues, the holy fools embody an unsettling reality of the gospel, which many of us are tempted to ignore. And that unsettling reality is this: Scandal is an essential part of the message. The holiness and the madness are quite simply inseparable. The naked street preachers, Murav argues, sought to make visible the image of God in its deeply scandalous form.[18]

In their one-man shows the holy fools staged what Murav calls the "problem of recognition."[19] They enacted a spectacle that was always, intentionally susceptible to a double interpretation—just like Jesus' scandalous life, death, and resurrection.[20] Through their carnivalesque street theater, the holy fools, including the naked street preachers, created a space that provoked people to learn to "look." They enacted events that challenged people to discern the gospel within the scandal—the holiness within the madness. It was all carefully staged to provoke a kind of looking, a way of "seeing."

The naked street preachers quite intentionally created a crisis of recognition, a crisis of decision. And usually they were abused and ridiculed because most people never discerned the holiness within the madness. As Murav writes, "The first step for the unrighteous, for those who are bored and do not know how to look ... is to be confounded."[21] Others, however, did discern the gospel within the scandal, and they were converted or edified.[22]

The hagiographies of these holy fools followed a similar pattern. In presenting the life of the fool, they too were inviting the reader to look; they were creating a crisis of recognition. At issue in the hagiographies is the reader's response. Were these people simply fools—or were they holy fools? Only those who knew how to "look" could dis-

18. Murav, *Holy Foolishness*, 49.

19. Ibid., 97.

20. Ibid., 96.

21. Ibid.

22. Ibid.

cern the gospel within the scandal. As Murav writes, "Holy foolishness is not a simple kind of sanctity but one that always foregrounds that which is problematic and confounds those who seek to categorize it. The hagiographer . . . represents the holy fool not as a simple innocent but as one who deliberately conceals his true nature from others by assuming a mask of folly. More specifically, the holy fool uses his secret knowledge to provoke and manipulate others."[23]

As Murav suggests in this quotation, things get even more confounding. For even when one learns to look, even when one recognizes the gospel within the scandal, there is still no separating the two. The holiness and the madness remain intertwined. You can never somehow remove the kernel of the gospel from the husk of the scandal. As a result, there is no way to categorize the gospel or gain control of it.

Again, in Murav's words: "The scandal is much more than a breach of decorum. It is that which cannot be mastered."[24] So even the apostle Paul, when he writes about preaching in First Corinthians, is left stammering about foolishness that is wisdom and weakness that is power, never able to disentangle the two, despite all our efforts to explain and master what he says (1 Cor 1:18–25).[25] Even Paul is left stammering about the *double* foolishness of preaching, which is not only the foolishness of the scandalous message itself, but the foolishness of trying to bring it to speech or master it through rhetoric. Perhaps that is why the naked street preachers would often mumble nonsensical speech as they engaged in their bizarre

23. Ibid., 93.

24. Ibid., 96.

25. Paul actually uses the Greek term, *skandalon*, when discussing the cross in 1 Corinthians 1:23.

street theater; they were reminding us of the limitations of words.

Murav's work brings me back to the place where this little adventure into foolishness and naked street preaching began. It all started with a short story by Fyodor Dostoevsky titled, "The Dream of a Ridiculous Man," which has become one of my favorite homiletics texts. The story opens with these words of the first-person narrator, which bring to mind the holy fools: "I am a ridiculous man. They call me a madman now."[26] So from the beginning we know the narrator is a madman, but we don't yet know if it's a holy madness or not. So he tells his story.

The ridiculous man (who is never named) had despaired of the world and given up on it. He had cut himself off completely from other human beings, even cruelly dismissing a poor, desperate young girl of the streets, who cries out for his help. In the midst of his cynicism and despair, on the verge of committing suicide, he falls asleep and has a dream (again, like the holy fools who often receive their instructions in dreams). In the dream he has a vision of salvation, a vision of the universal harmony of shalom. But in the dream, this salvation becomes corrupted. And the corruption cannot be overcome because there is no Christ; there is no crucifixion or resurrection. As a result there is no hope. The vision cannot become reality in the dream.

When the ridiculous man awakes, however, he realizes that his vision of salvation can come to fulfillment on earth because Christ has come here. In this sense, the earth—human history with all of its anguish and suffering and

26. Dostoevsky, "A Ridiculous Man," 263.

corruption—is a place of more hope than the dream.[27] When the ridiculous man awakes to this realization, he longs for life. But that is not all. He also desires something more. In rather typical melodramatic Dostoevskian fashion, the ridiculous man exclaims,

> Oh, how I longed for life, life! I lifted up my hands and called upon eternal Truth—no, not called upon it, but wept. Rapture, infinite boundless rapture intoxicated me. Yes, life and . . . [and here's the something more] . . . life and—preaching. I made up my mind to preach from that very moment and, of course, to go on preaching all my life. I am going to preach, I want to preach. What? Why, truth. For I have beheld truth, I have beheld it with my own eyes, I have beheld it in all its glory.[28]

Life and preaching become one for the ridiculous man; he has learned to look, he has seen the truth, and now he must preach.

But there's only one problem. He cannot find the words. He simply cannot categorize or master what he has seen. And everyone ridicules him and laughs at him—just as they ridiculed the naked street preachers. As he states at the beginning, "They call me a madman now"—now that he is preaching. And he draws us into the anguish of preaching— the anguish of trying to proclaim a word in which holiness and madness are essentially and inseparably related. "I do not know how to put it into words," he says. "After my dream I lost the knack of putting things into words. At least, into the

27. This interpretation is drawn from Thompson, "Problems of the Biblical Word in Dostoevsky's Poetics," 86.

28. Dostoevsky, "A Ridiculous Man," 283–84.

most necessary and important words. But never mind. I shall go on and I shall keep on talking, for I have indeed beheld it with my own eyes, though I cannot describe what I saw."[29] Exasperated, he finally exclaims, "The main thing is to love your neighbor as yourself—that is the main thing, and that is everything, for nothing else matters."[30] But even that exclamation sounds rather ridiculous in the context. So, as with most of Dostoevsky's fools, we're left to decide: Is the ridiculous man *just* a fool—or is he a holy fool?

I think this is the drama the naked street preachers enact in the midst of their madness. They set before us the very heart of preaching: that foolish and unruly gospel that cannot be categorized or mastered; that foolish and unruly gospel that leaves us stammering like ridiculous people when we really try to put it into words: "Foolishness is wisdom and weakness is power." Through their bizarre antics, the naked street preachers set before us the heart of preaching, which, to be honest, even homiletics can never master. And I wonder if that is why the naked street preachers have been virtually ignored in homiletics—maybe they're just too threatening to our theories and our frameworks.

In fact, these figures are threatening to those of us who are called to teach preaching. Indeed, they may represent the homiletical "other" who profoundly challenges us. For they remind us that, in the deepest sense, preaching cannot be taught. Joseph Sittler made this point many years ago in his extraordinary little book, *The Anguish of Preaching*. As he wrote in now widely-quoted words, "the expectation must not be cherished that, save for modest and obvious instruction

29. Ibid., 285.
30. Ibid.

about voice, pace, organization, and such matters, preaching as a lively art of the church can be taught at all. And therefore, seminary provisions for instruction in preaching . . . should be re-examined."[31]

The naked street preachers likewise expose the foolishness of homileticians: we're called to teach something that cannot really be taught. For all the books and all the theories and all the lectures and all the directives of homileticians can never categorize or master the gospel that we preach. We can teach about transitions and unity and movement and language. We can help students develop the homiletical tools of exegesis and hermeneutics and theology. And we can work with them on speech and delivery and performance. And all of that is valuable; it can help people prepare and deliver better sermons. But, as most of us know, all of that rolled up beautifully together—all of that done perfectly—does not equal *preaching*.

Teaching preaching is in some ways utter folly. For all the wisdom of homiletics cannot bring someone to faith or enable someone to look. All the wisdom of homiletics cannot teach someone the foolishness—the scandal—of the gospel. And even for preachers who learn to "look," even for those who "get" the scandal, all the homiletical insights in the world can never tell them how to capture what they see in words.

And many of my students already know all of this. I can't fool them. They look around at what passes for wisdom and power in the world, and they know the gospel is foolishness. They know that even in the church the gospel often appears ridiculous. And they know that preaching is the place where they have to come to terms with this madness; preaching is

31. Sittler, *Anguish of Preaching*, 7.

the place where they are left standing naked before the gospel, being confounded and claimed all at the same time. They may try to distance themselves from this foolishness in the rest of their lives and even the rest of their studies, but when they have to preach, they often cannot maintain the distance.

One of my students, Sarah Walker, named this experience for some of us, and she has given me permission to share part of her sermon. She was reflecting on her efforts to keep her distance from the insanity of the gospel texts. She said:

> It works out really well, this distancing, until you make me preach. Preaching is becoming the bane of my existence. I can get through all my other classes, through the rest of my life, without having to *really* face the claims of the text. But you ask me to preach and I just can't avoid them. I can distance myself from the texts in my life, but I can't get up and preach distance. . . . So I am slammed in the face with these texts—with the implausible promises and the injunctions to do the insane.

Afterward, a number other students commented, "That's it . . . That's it."

Many of my students know exactly what it's like to be that ridiculous person, seeing the holy madness of the gospel and stammering to put it into words. They know the nakedness that inevitably comes with preaching. And they don't want me trying to pawn off on them a gospel that fits neatly into a homiletics text or a focus and function statement. They don't want me to try to dress up their nakedness in Sunday finery so they will be respectable and presentable, like harmless little dolls in a toy store where churches go shopping for pastors. They want something real, even if it is ridiculous. They want to wrestle with this gospel in all of its scandal. They want a gospel that is big enough and unruly enough to confound and claim their lives over and over again—even if stammering to preach it drives them crazy. And, frankly, I think that's also precisely the kind of gospel and the kind of preacher our churches desperately need today.

Along with the naked street preachers, these students push me toward a more extreme homiletic, one that moves beyond traditional homiletical categories and theories. Here, at least in part, is what I think I'm hearing. Don't worry so much about teaching preaching. Focus instead on forming preachers. Help students learn to look—to discern the folly of the crucified and risen Word in the text, in their lives, in the church, and in the world. Create spaces where that scandalous gospel might confound and claim them. And then walk with them into those spaces and stand with them as they stammer trying to bring that gospel to speech. In short, accompany your students as they become ridiculous people, who bet their lives on a scandalous Word that they can never fully form into words.

It is foolishness really. The preaching, the teaching, the whole thing. But it is also the power of God and the wisdom of God for salvation.

5

Preacher as Fisher

Lincoln E. Galloway

---

¹⁶ As Jesus passed along the Sea of Galilee, he saw Simon and his brother Andrew casting a net into the sea—for they were fishermen. ¹⁷And Jesus said to them, "Follow me and I will make you fish for people." ¹⁸And immediately they left their nets and followed him. ¹⁹As he went a little farther, he saw James son of Zebedee and his brother John, who were in their boat mending the nets. ²⁰Immediately he called them; and they left their father Zebedee in the boat with the hired men, and followed him. (Mark 1:16–20)

IN CARIBBEAN life, one is constantly aware of the sea and the wide array of activities related to the sea. The sea provides a clear demarcation of each island and yet provides a unique bond from shore to shore. The sea has its own rhythmic patterns that seem to resonate with the musical soul and consciousness of Caribbean culture. The beauty of the sea, its myriad colors, and caressing waves provide an irresistible lure for both residents as well as visitors. In one season, the sea may be tranquil, calm and serene providing an idyllic backdrop for a tropical paradise. In another season, its gloomy foreboding is a harbinger to storms, in the form of hurricanes that force the waters to roar, and the waves to crash upon the shore with immeasurable force.

Through all of its movements, the sea continues to captivate us for its treasures of unexplored bounty and as a source of daily sustenance. I recall my own experience of seeing fishermen at work in their boats or pulling their nets to shore, while on the beach were the multitudes waiting to buy fish, as well as those preoccupied with their recreational activities in sand and surf. Among other things, the sea represents for Caribbean people recreation and delight, work and sustenance, exploration and danger, as well as intrigue and mystery. In light of the ubiquitous presence and significant role of the sea in Caribbean life, I wanted to explore the biblical record for a trope that would have some resonance with the cultural world of Caribbean people.

One place of resonance with Caribbean life is in Mark's Gospel where the sea provides the spatial world for significant aspects of Jesus' ministry. It provides the venue, stage, and backdrop for some of the narratives about Jesus' ministry. In the Gospel, the sea is not only beautiful natural scenery that is passive and inconsequential, its role is significant and on occasion the sea is an active, dynamic, presence with its own unique role as an actor in the unfolding drama. Jesus encounters fishers at the sea who will become his disciples. For these disciples, the sea is the source of their livelihood, a place of investment, employment, and hard work (Mark 1:16–20). At times, the sea is a place of retreat where Jesus can escape from the crowds so that he is not crushed (Mark 3:7–10). At other times, the sea is a place where people gather and Jesus could teach a very large crowd (Mark 4:1–2). The sea is transformed by Jesus' presence and actions in the midst of a storm (Mark 4:35–41); and the sea is the place where the words and actions of Jesus inspire awe and astonishment (Mark 6:45–51). In these Markan narratives, Jesus transforms the sea, a place of industry, into a place of teaching; and a place of chaos, into a place of divine epiphany.

Unlike Caribbean people who regard the sea as a heavenly foretaste, the Markan world probably shared the apocalyptic expectation of a time when the sea would be no more.[1] The world painted by Mark's narrative contains echoes of the Hebrew bible in which the sea epitomizes the chaos that must be contained and directed by the creative activity of God.[2] The sea is the arena for an ongoing drama which celebrates divine power and conquest over the chaos. The psalmist can declare: "The sea is his, for he made it . . ." (Ps 95:5). Then in praise to God who is great, awesome, mighty and faithful: "You rule the raging of the sea; when its waves rise, you still them" (Ps 89:9). The sea evokes images of cosmic disorder and chaos, but it also emerges as a place of mystery, intrigue, and divine activity. Mark's gospel draws our interest to the role of the sea and also invites us to pay close attention to Jesus' relationship to the sea. There is alarm and anxiety as the curtain is lifted, the stage is revealed and the drama begins. The world of Jesus' ministry is brought into view and highlighted by this Markan description: "Again he began to teach beside *the sea*. Such a very large crowd gathered around him that he got into a boat

---

1. "Then I saw a new heaven and a new earth; for the first heaven and the first earth had passed away, and the sea was no more" (Rev 21:1).

2. Genesis 1:6–10; Psalm 107:23–29.

on *the sea* and sat there, while the crowd was beside *the sea* on the land" (Mark 4:1).

With the sea as the stage or backdrop in the Gospel of Mark, the trope of *preacher as fisher* emerges as we stand with the disciples and experience the life and ministry of Jesus. In the midst of their work, some would-be disciples first encounter Jesus at the sea and he says to them: "Follow me and I will make you fish for people" (Mark 1:17). The word play of Jesus is grounded in the everyday reality and life experiences of people who engaged in fishing for a livelihood, and who tried in their own ways to understand the ways of the sea. Jesus' invitation highlights the full vocational context of these first disciples whose lives revolve around the sea, fish, nets, and boats. These aspects, implements or tools of the fisher's world had immediate applicability to the message of Jesus. They were based in everyday life and able to generate useful images for communicating some aspects of Christian faith and teaching. As Elizabeth Rees indicates the evidence is found in the underground catacomb paintings with images of doves, sheep and lambs with shepherds among others, but also fishers with their nets and rods: "As followers of Christ they saw themselves as doves and shepherded lambs, as fish caught in the net of the Church."[3] These images drawn from the sea and the life of fishing would spark imaginations and

---

3. Rees, *Christian Symbols,* 20. She writes that, "In some paintings of the Baptism of Jesus, fish or little people or both are swimming in the Jordan. The fish represent Christians who will be baptized in the wake of Jesus. Sometimes, as at Sant Apollinare Nuovo in Ravenna, apostles sailing in the ship of the Church cast their net to catch fish, who again represent new believers, since Jesus told his friends, 'I will make you fishers of men' . . ." (97).

remain as enduring symbols that the Christian church would wrestle with across the centuries.[4]

The trope of *preacher as fisher* is not without its problems for the field of homiletics and for the preacher of the twenty-first century. The first and most glaring difficulty with the trope is that the term "fisherman" used in everyday parlance is gender exclusive speech. Such gender exclusive terms reflect a world in which men make decisions about households and business enterprises. This is the social fabric exhibited in the Gospel story around persons beside the sea who own homes and have family commitments (Mark 1:29) and obligations to the hired hands who assist in their fishing business (Mark 1:20). However, in our contemporary society, communication is readily impeded by the use of gender exclusive terms.[5]

4. In Christian art and design, the sea is easily associated with the waters of baptism and fish as Christians who will be baptized. These symbols of sea, fish, nets and boats have endured through the centuries beginning with some of the earliest paintings in catacombs and represented in modern designs in churches today. See Child and Colles, *Christian Symbols, Ancient & Modern*. As a modern example, Child and Colles depict a font in the church of the Epiphany at Corby, designed in 1962 with several symbols. Among them is a seedling symbolizing birth and development. "Above the seedling is a fish—the ancient sign of Baptism" (108–9). The fish in early Christian iconography bears witness to the ways in which the world of the first disciples evoked creative ways to express Christian teaching. The use of the *ichthys* symbol by early Christians appears to date from the end of the first century CE. The acronym *ichthys* was created by combining the first letters of several words to form ΙΧΘΥΣ (Greek for fish) from "Jesus Christ God's Son Savior."

5. Several texts deal with this issue with special reference to the theological disciplines of preaching and worship. See Wren, *What Language Shall I Borrow?* and McFague, *Metaphorical Theology*.

The second difficulty is that, unlike images such as shepherd (Ezek 34:11–31) or nurse (1 Thess 2:3–8), fishing conjures a climate of fear.[6] The fisher's tools are hooks, spears, and nets; implements that violently snare, entrap, and entangle.[7] These tools of the trade are not easily reconcilable with Christian proclamation or Gospel. Further, the audience is implicitly invited to identify with fish and this poses further hermeneutical difficulties. Among these is the notion that the audience is pursued, captured, and dragged ashore without any consideration given to individual thought, desire, will, responsiveness, or agency. The trope of *preacher as fisher* is undoubtedly rooted in the biblical narrative, Christian teaching and consciousness, paintings and designs. However, it is also one that will invite debate and pose certain limitations and pitfalls in its use.

As the Markan narrative unfolds, Jesus encounters fishers (brothers Simon and Andrew) as they are casting their

6. The image of the preacher as a nurse is used by Paul to contrast his proclamation and that of his colleagues with that of other orators whose words spring from impure motives and who may employ tricks or flattery in their speeches. Abraham Malherbe's analysis of 1 Thessalonians 2 indicates that Paul employs similar images and terminology to describe appropriate speech as used by moral philosophers in Greco-Roman literature. See Malherbe, "'Gentle as a Nurse,'" 203–17.

7. The proclamation against Pharaoh, king of Egypt and against all Egypt: "I will put hooks in your jaws, and make the fish of your channels stick to your scales" (Ezek 29:4). To the "cows of Bashan who are on Mount Samaria, who oppress the poor, who crush the needy . . . The time is surely coming upon you when they shall take you away with hooks, even the last of you with fishhooks" (Amos 4:1–2). "You have made people like crawling things that have no ruler. The enemy brings all of them up with a hook; he drags them out with his net, he gathers them in his seine . . . Is he then to keep on emptying his net, and destroying nations without mercy?" (Hab 3:14–17).

nets into the sea, and (the sons of Zebedee, brothers James and John) in their boat mending their nets (Mark 1:16–19). The fishers are invited to fish for people. This play on the occupational title is not applied to Levi sitting at the tax booth. Jesus speaks briefly to Levi: "'Follow me.' And he got up and followed him" (Mark 2:13–14). Some have suggested that this play with the fishers was possible because the notion of fishing for people had become popular in Greek life as a metaphor for the activity of moral philosophers.[8] If these first disciples understood the ramifications of this metaphor, then these fishers left their families and professions knowing, at the very least, that they were being called to a life of virtue.

For Mark, it is significant that the fishers, portrayed in the context of the obligations of family and business, are summoned by Jesus. It is Jesus who comes to the sea. It is Jesus who sees them as they were ("for they were fishers"). It is Jesus who calls them. Mark does not provide a good reason why they should follow. There is no narrative about a large miraculous catch of fish to provide a context for the call or a motive to prompt a response (cf. Luke 5:1–11). In Mark, the disciples will witness miracles of healing and feeding and still appear unable to perceive the divine at work in the One in their midst. However, in this instance, the call of Jesus is enough (cf. 1 Kgs 19:19–21). They accept Jesus' summons with all of its ramifications for family and business obligations.

The story holds a summons or command, a promise, and a response. Jesus promises them that they will fish for

---

8. In Hellenistic literature, there are similar stories of the philosopher-teacher calling disciples to leave everything and follow. See Berger, Boring, and Colpe, *Hellenistic Commentary to the New Testament*; and Wuellner, *The Meaning of "Fishers of Men."*

people. In this act, we are reminded once again that it is Jesus who has taken the initiative. In the command: "Follow me," is an invitation to discipleship. With the invitation comes an explicit promise: "I will make you fish for people." The Gospel narrative has put before us a call story constructed around notions of command or invitation, and promise. It calls attention to the nature of commitment in a manner that invites the readers to find themselves in the story. Sometimes, like the crowds portrayed in the Gospel, we are amazed. We are amazed that the disciples actually follow. We are amazed that like them, we also listen for and hear that invitation. We are amazed that like them, the call of Jesus is enough, and we are willing to accept Jesus' summons with all its ramifications for our families and our business obligations.

The disciples were immediately to share the stage with Jesus. This would be their story because they would from now on be doing what only Jesus could do. The invitation to fish for people is not to an obscure apprenticeship but to a participation in the life and work of the maestro. They would be infected by the same spirit that drove him into the wilderness (Mark 1:12); and by which he cast out demons and healed the sick (Mark 1:34). "So they went out and proclaimed that all should repent. They cast out many demons, and anointed with oil many who were sick and cured them" (Mark 6:12–13). The disciples were experiencing a new way of being in the world and that would also include a new way of experiencing the sea.

The call to fish for people carries the promise of divine epiphany. By showing what they often missed, Mark challenges those who are summoned by Jesus, invited to fish for people, those who follow Jesus, to recognize God's presence and power at work in Jesus. The storms will come. These fishers knew about them. So, when a great windstorm arose, their terror is palpable. They awaken Jesus from his sleep to ask if he does not care about them.[9] In the ensuing sequence of events, we hear echoes of Psalm 107: "He made the storm be still, and the waves of the sea were hushed" (107:29). In speaking peace to the storm so that there was a dead calm, Jesus demonstrates that the divine presence that restrains the chaotic waters was working in him. This revelation may have caused cognitive dissonance for the fishers as they say to one another, "who then is this, that even the wind and the sea obey him?" (Mark 4:35–41). The fishers were learning that following Jesus would challenge their understandings of divine presence and activity. In order to fish for people, they also had to learn how to interpret the work of Jesus among them. Jesus had called them just as they were. On that day, when evening had come, they had taken Jesus "with them in the boat, just as he was." How was he? Was he in garments unfit for the sea? Had he succumbed to fatigue because of the overwhelming needs of the crowd? Was he using their boat for rest, while those in the other boats with him were on a fishing expedition? What we do know is that a complete and immediate calm ensues and the disciples are filled with great awe.

Many of us, who read the Gospel of Mark in the twenty-first century, are aware of the many recreational activities that are associated with the sea. The sport of water-skiing is perhaps the closest activity to walking on water. On this occasion, the boat was out on the sea, and the disciples were straining at the oars against an adverse wind. Readers find this story

9. In Matthew's Gospel they plead for help: "Lord, save us!" (Matt 8:25).

intriguing because we already know of Jesus' power over the wind and the waves of the sea (Mark 4:35–41). The story is even more intriguing because it was Jesus who had "made his disciples get into the boat and go on ahead to the other side" (Mark 6:45). We do not know what method of transportation Jesus would use in order to join them on the other side. We can surmise that this would be a moment of recreation for Jesus and that he was planning to have a little fun with them and ski right pass them. However that plan had to be aborted because the disciples were too terrified. Jesus had to speak words of assurance to them and get into the boat with them.

The *preacher as fisher* is a trope that is fraught with problems and yet it has wonderful possibilities for preachers and for the field of homiletics, not least of which is the template it provides for a call story. The preacher as fisher responds to a call to follow Jesus. In such a call story, there is the recognition that Jesus takes the initiative, enters into our everyday experiences, and speaks into our context. Since Jesus transforms places of industry into places of learning, places of recreation into places of divine epiphany, places of chaos into places of awe and wonder, the preacher as fisher is invited to continually interpret the words and actions of Jesus. The fisher is invited to sit with Jesus in the boat in the places of chaos and uncertainty, where good and evil are in a constant struggle, and where the familiar encounters the unfamiliar. The fisher sits over the deep with repeated opportunities to ponder the unknown, to experience occasional terror, and to stand amazed at the ways in which our encounters with Jesus call forth an unfolding witness to the awesome presence of God.

6

Preacher as Host and Guest

JOHN S. McCLURE[1]

THE PRACTICE of extending hospitality to the stranger or guest has ancient roots within the Judeo-Christian tradition. Abraham, the "wandering Aramean" (Deut 26:5) was dependent on hosts who were Canaanite and Egyptian, and was hosted by Melchizedek, king of Salem (Genesis 14).[2] In Genesis 18, we are told that Abraham hosted three very significant strangers who informed Sarah she would bear a child late in life. As *gērîm* (sojourners), the people of Israel knew in no uncertain terms the importance of the host-guest relationship. It was a key to survival and became increasingly important in discerning and articulating the nature of faith. After

1. Brief portions of this essay are adapted from my book *The Roundtable Pulpit*, 13–29.

2. I will not make philosophical distinctions between "degrees of stranger-ness" such as those made by Hermann Cohen, who distinguishes between the "next man" toward whom we are basically indifferent, the "stranger" who is "potentially hostile," the "guest-friend" toward whom one is "obligated," and the "fellowman" with whom we are "lovingly engaged." Emerson, "Foreword," xiii. Scripture makes no such distinctions, and we assume that all of these degrees of stranger-ness are potentialities in any stranger/guest.

the sojourn in Egypt, an ethic of hospitality developed within Israel, through which Israel's experiences as guest informed their experience of themselves as hosts. This culminated in the well-known ethical mandate articulated in Deuteronomy 10:19, "You shall also love the stranger, for you were strangers in the land of Egypt." This ethic of hospitality became an important aspect of both social and household life.

Theologian Amos Yong, in *Hospitality and the Other: Pentecost, Christian Practices, and the Neighbor,* chronicles the life of Jesus as a "paradigm of hospitality."[3] From his birth in a manger to his burial by Joseph of Arimathea, Jesus was "dependent on the welcome of others," and was a guest of Simon Peter, Levi, Martha, Zacchaeus, as well as Pharisees and others left unnamed.[4] Luke portrays Jesus pushing back against misuses of the rules of hospitality when his host seemed to be using the rules of hospitality to silence his voice (Luke 11:37–41).[5] Often, as guest, Jesus changes roles and becomes the host of a conversation focused on discerning a new truth. Luke's story of the Road to Emmaus is paradigmatic of this host-guest reversal (Luke 24:13–35). In that story Jesus the charismatic stranger is hosted and then in a startling moment of reversal and recognition becomes host (v. 31).

New Testament scholar Michael White, in an important study of social authority in the early Christian churches, argues that charismatic apostles such as Paul and Peter showed deference to the traditional authority of the host within the

---

3. Yong, *Hospitality and the Other,* 101.

4. Ibid., 101.

5. Ibid., 102. See also Gowler, "Hospitality and Characterization in Luke 11:37–54."

family household.[6] Because the earliest Christian congregations met in homes, authority was vested in familial activities of hospitality. White shows how the social conventions of hospitality and patronage were well developed in the early church and included "receiving . . . preaching, mutual exhortation, and communal fellowship around the dinner table which also served as the center of eucharistic anamnesis," and "sending on one's way."[7] In Philippians (1:5; 4:15) Paul calls such actions of hospitality partnership (*koinōnia*) in the gospel. Elsewhere they are called acts of service (*diakonia*) and expressions of love (*agapē*) (Rom 16:1–2; Philemon 4–6). In addition to the house churches that served primarily upper- or middle-class Christians, there were also "tenement churches" which "consisted entirely of the urban underclass, primarily slaves and former slaves."[8] Hosting in these churches appears to have been shared among several co-hosts. Romans 16:15, for instance, refers to five such hosts: Philologus, Julia, Nereus, Nereus's sister, and Olympas, whose names indicate that they were slaves or former slaves.[9]

The itinerant, charismatic (gift-bearing) prophet was always and by necessity hosted. Paul was hosted by many: Judas on the Straight Street, Ananias, those who helped him escape from enemies, Barnabas, Lydia, the Philippian jailer, Jason of Thessalonica, Prisca and Aquilla, Titius Justus, Philip the

---

6. See White, "Social Authority in the House Church Setting."

7. Ibid., 215, 217.

8. Jewett, *Paul: Apostle to America*, 80.

9. According to Robert Jewett, Philologus and Julia probably represented members of a shared leadership cadre in the early tenement churches, ibid., 80.

evangelist, Mnason, and other unnamed disciples.[10] According to New Testament scholar John Koenig, by the end of Acts, Paul had become "both itinerant and resident, guest and host, minister of the word and minister of the table."[11] This fluidity of roles meant that the community welcomed and permitted itself to be constantly instructed by charismatic individuals from within and beyond its boundaries. According to Koenig, the entire sweep of Luke-Acts "is aimed at building up local leadership so that it can strengthen the whole church *for partnership with the wandering prophets.*"[12] Luke emphasizes "a cooperative missionary effort characterized by a *fluidity in guest and host roles.*"[13]

A NEW IMAGE FOR THE PREACHER

When searching among images from the New Testament for the preacher, homileticians have traditionally focused more attention on images that undergird itinerant and charismatic pulpit ministry, especially the images of herald, prophet, fool, and witness. Each of these has an important function in Scripture and within the homiletical tradition. It may be

10. For more detail on this list, see *Yong, Hospitality and the Other,* 104.

11. Koenig, *New Testament Hospitality,* 109.

12. Ibid., 98.

13. Ibid., 119, emphasis added. Stories such as the sinful woman's anointing of Jesus' feet, the parable of the Good Samaritan, the parable of the prodigal son, the stories of Mary and Martha and Zacchaeus and many others demonstrate the importance of the guest-host theme in Luke's writing. In Acts there appears to be more emphasis on the hosts who become "residential prophets" (2:1–4; 11:27–30; 13:1–3; 15:32–35; 19:1–7; 21:8–9; 21:10).

helpful, however, for parish-based, congregation-centered preachers to look to Barnabas and Phoebe, Philologus and Julia, or the disciples on the road to Emmaus, for an image of the nature and authority of the preacher within the Christian community. The contemporary parish preacher could see the preaching ministry, at least in part, as an act of hospitality.

In the first instance, the preacher, like the disciples on the road to Emmaus, is a *host* who welcomes strangers into the preaching ministry. As hosts, we welcome all with a word to share into dialogue so that the word and wisdom of God might be discerned for the community.

In the second instance, the preacher, like the disciples on the Road to Emmaeus, becomes guest. As we host charismatic (gift-bearing) guests who "open scriptures" in striking new ways (Luke 24:32), we find ourselves suddenly guests, hosted by others.

Broadening the Congregation: Five Ways to Think of "Strangers"

There are at least five ways to think of the strangers we host. First, and most foundationally, the stranger signifies what liturgical theologian Patrick Kiefert calls "the irreducible difference between two persons that exists in any encounter."[14] Theologian Edward Farley calls this the "mysterious presence of something which contests my projecting meanings on it, an unforeseeable depth which . . . cannot be cognitively or emotionally mastered."[15]

14. Kiefert, *Welcoming the Stranger*, 8–9.
15. Farley, *Good and Evil*, 39.

Second, the stranger represents those who come from outside the religious community itself, from beyond geographic, racial, ethnic, or religious boundaries. This was true of Melchizedek of Salem, a Canaanite priest of El Elyon, and "the High-priest of the cosmic religion,"[16] who was hosted by Abraham. According to Yong, the stranger in this perspective represents "how the religious longings and perhaps even beliefs and practices of all people are oriented toward God ..."[17]

Third, the stranger represents those inside the religious community inasmuch as aspects of their lives remain strangers to, or estranged from, the community's self-awareness and the discernment of its immediate mission and witness. Luke's gospel is filled with stories about the healing hospitality of Jesus toward these strangers: the man with an unclean spirit (4:31–37), the man with a withered hand (6:6–11), the woman who was a sinner (7:36–50), and the man with leprosy (14:1–6). In our context this might include parishioners such as Mildred, who at age seventy with no children is lonely, but keeps this to herself at church. Or there is Susan, a lesbian, who keeps her sexuality "under wraps." There is Bob who was abused as a child and struggles with the idea of forgiveness. There is Rebecca, a twelve year old whose parents recently divorced, now confused about the meaning of love. And there is Carl, a single parent of three children, who barely survives at the bottom of the pay scale and works hard to maintain appearances. Although many aspects of the lives of these individuals are welcome in church, other

16. Daniélou, *Holy Pagans of the Old Testament*, 104; quoted in Yong, *Hospitality and the Other*, 117.

17. Ibid.

aspects remain strangers, not fully welcomed in the discernment of the meaning of the gospel.

Fourth, the stranger represents those who have been in the community of faith but are either leaving it or have already departed. These are people estranged from the church for any number of reasons—intentionally strangers. They may feel wounded by the church, or simply find the church irrelevant to their daily lives.

Finally, the stranger represents all the ways in which we are "strangers to ourselves." Each of us is not a unitary or solitary self but a community of selves in conversation. Many of our own inner selves remain voiceless within, not allowed to participate fully in the conversation that shapes our identity as Christians.

When one considers this "company of strangers"[18] as the preacher's congregation, we can see that, although not removing the boundary between the religious community and culture, hospitality softens the borders, and allows for more fluidity between "inside" and "outside." Strangers are not just outside. They are inside, and when all is said and done, inside strangers and outside strangers are usually deeply connected. The preacher as host and guest, therefore, always prepares and preaches sermons (at least figuratively) at the church door, within this larger company of strangers.

18. See Palmer, *The Company of Strangers*. The company of strangers for Palmer is a metaphor for the "public life" where we encounter strangers. This public life is vital to faith as "a venture into the unknown, into the realms of mystery, away from the safe and comfortable and secure" (56).

THE AUTHORITY OF THE PREACHER AS HOST AND GUEST

Historically, the authority of the preacher derives from many sources: office, ordination, scripture, professional competence, charisma, celebrity, and so on. While any or all of these may be at work, the primary form of authority for the preacher as host and guest is what practical theologian Jackson Carroll calls "relational authority."[19] In the 1980s and 1990s, the inductive and narrative preaching movements made good use of relational authority within forms of preaching which encouraged relational *symmetry* between preacher and congregation. In ways similar to Kenneth Burke's rhetorical theory, which focused on the need to achieve rhetorical "consubstantiality,"[20] preachers were encouraged to *identify* with listeners. The goal of the sermon was to take the listener on a shared inductive or narrative journey with the preacher.

Relational symmetry in the pulpit, however, has its limitations. The primary problem issues from the idea of relational *symmetry* itself: the preacher's assumption that he or she can and indeed must identify with listeners, using forms of empathic imagination. The inductive preacher assumes that experiences are largely interchangeable. Sermon ideas and illustrations are built on an assumed common form of experience.

For the preacher as host and guest, however, relational authority is conceived differently. The authority of the preacher is undergirded by a deep sense of relational *asymmetry*. The

19. Carroll, *As One With Authority*, 61–78. For more on relational asymmetry, see Ogletree, *Hospitality to the Stranger*, 35–63.

20. Burke, *A Rhetoric of Motives*.

preacher as host and guest does not assume the dominance of common human experience, and avoids treating experiences of God as somehow interchangeable. This would deny the differences between our experiences of God, precluding the gifts that strangers bring to the discernment of God's presence in the world. Although there may be momentary identifications between conversation partners, establishing common ground, it is *difference* that starts conversations and keeps them going in pursuit of truth. The preacher as host and guest values this difference and the deferring of ultimate truth that comes from being part of an open-ended conversation. Authority, then, issues less from the fact that the preacher is "like me" and speaks "my language," and more from the fact that the preacher speaks first *with* me, and is then granted the authority to speak *for* or *to* me.

Five Clarifications about Authority

The authority of the preacher as host and guest is easily misunderstood. Five things should be made clear about asymmetrical relational authority. First, it is *kenotic* authority. There will be some for whom the preacher as host and guest seems to invite a diminution or dereliction of the preacher's authority or what sociologists, following Max Weber, call "legitimate power."[21] As New Testament scholar John Howard Schütz demonstrates in *Paul and the Anatomy of Apostolic Authority*, this sociological view of authority is inappropriate to the New Testament context. Authority in the early church

21. See Talcott Parson's notes on the translation of the word "power" in Max Weber, *The Theory of Social and Economic Organization*, 152, n. 83. See also Weber, *Economy and Society*, vols. 1–2.

is best understood as the result of a particular "interpretation of power," a process of negotiating an "interpretative framework, in the form of a master narrative or a pregnant constellation of metaphors, that makes sense of power that they themselves may experience or have experienced."[22] The most fundamental interpretive framework with respect to issues of power in relation to others, is found in Philippians 2:1–11. This hymn to Christ encourages us to see our authority as preachers grounded in Christ's ministry as one who chose not to "regard equality with God as something to be exploited, but emptied himself" (2:6–7a). As feminist scholars have shown, Christ's "kenosis," or "emptying" of himself unto death does not foist upon us a masochistic refusal of selfhood or the authority to speak with legitimate prophetic and pastoral power.[23] Authority after the pattern of Christ, however, is shaped

22. Wayne A. Meeks, "Introduction," xxi. In a similar manner, Thomas Csordas argues that charisma "is rhetoric . . . a particular mode of interpersonal efficacy: not a quality, but a collective, performative, intersubjective self process." Csordas, *Language, Charisma, and Creativity*, 140. As James Dunn observes, this authority was a function, ultimately of discipleship or being "totally bound to Jesus' person and his mission . . . It was only as they shared in his mission that his disciples shared in his authority and charismatic power." Dunn, *Jesus and the Spirit*, 81.

23. See, for instance Hampson, "On Power and Gender," 234–35. The view encouraged here, however, might be closer to that articulated by Coakley in "Kenosis and Subversion," and in Coakley, "Kenosis." Whereas Hampson rejects kenosis as inappropriate or even dangerous for women, especially in situations of abuse, Coakley works to unite "human 'vulnerability' with authentic divine power . . . and uniting them such that the human was wholly translucent to the divine," "Kenosis," 95. Aristotle Papanikolaou calls this "a non-grasping at worldly forms of power in order to make oneself available to the true empowerment that comes through the presence of divine power." Papanikolaou, "Person, *Kenosis* and Abuse," 45.

by a refusal to grasp forms of "omni-power" (omnipotence, omniscience, omnipresence) that may belong to God, and rejects autocratic or authoritarian forms of power that "lord it over" others—even in the name of prophetic speech and action (Mark 10:42). As Eastern Orthodox theologian Aristotle Papanikolaou points out, authority after the pattern of Christ is shaped by a *relational kenosis* modeled after the Trinity in which moving kenotically toward the other is fundamental to receiving "sources of empowerment" (love, trust, friendship, care) from the other.[24]

Second, authority within the bounds of hospitality is plurivocal, not univocal in nature. In the picture Michael White paints of the early church, the host constantly welcomed into conversation others within and beyond the community who claimed to have insights into the nature of the Christian message. When an individual spoke a message that was meant for the congregation, it was welcomed as potentially significant for the community's task of discerning the truth of the gospel. Even when these individuals preached a message contrary to the gospel (the law-observant evangelists at Galatia or the hedonists at Corinth) their message was allowed to be heard and was engaged in debate. This was permitted because the truth of the gospel was experienced as dynamic, emerging each day in open dialogue and debate. Truth was not narrow and exclusive, identified solely with one voice, one interpretation, or one leader. The host gained authority, not by speaking in one voice, but by *listening to*, and then *speaking in* many voices.

Plurivocal models of speech have the potential to shepherd preachers through one key impasse caused by univocal

24. Papanikolaou, "Person, *Kenosis* and Abuse", 56.

speech in today's cultural context. Increasingly, legitimate power to speak is granted only when one positions oneself as a univocal speaker within mutually opposed dualities or "binaries" such as insider-outsider, black-white, rich-poor, liberal-conservative, Democrat-Republican, center-margin, etc.[25] This univocal rhetoric of opposition has become central to the competitive marketplace of ideas within the media in late modern capitalist societies, in which ratings drive the dynamics between news outlets, talk shows and websites. In this situation, oppositional rhetoric is good for business. Subversive agency, counterculture, and counter cultural speech have become *commodified* and useful in the marketing of products.[26] It is likely that popular homiletic models fueled by ideas of univocal oppositional or counter-cultural speech both benefit from and perpetuate this cultural dynamic.[27] Sociologist James Block points out that this kind of univocal authority is rooted in romantic and modernist notions of selves as free, potentially subversive agents.[28] As free speaking agents we each have (or must find) one true (or righteous), and distinct (authentic) voice and our words find authority

25. Deconstructionist philosopher Jacques Derrida calls this "One + n" discourse, which presumes a "center" ("One") and "margins" ("n" or "supplement"). Derrida calls the "One + n" framework an "auto-immune" system which "makes violence of itself, does violence to itself and keeps itself from the other," Derrida, "Faith and Knowledge," 66.

26. See Horkheimer and Adorno, "The Culture Industry," 120–24. See also Frank and Weiland, *Commodify Your Dissent*; and Frank, *Business Culture, Counterculture, and the Rise of Hip Consumerism*.

27. See especially the very popular book by Willimon and Hauerwas, *Resident Aliens*.

28. See Block, "National Revival as the Crucible of Agency Character," 369–423. See also Ted Smith's analysis of sincerity in Finney's preaching in Smith, *The New Measures*.

by becoming part of communities of one true (or righteous), and distinct (authentic) voice. Authority in this framework derives primarily from being a clear and consistent mouthpiece for one of several competing monologues.

The fluid guest-host logic of hospitality works to disrupt this kind of monological authority without sacrificing the preacher's ability to resist and subvert various forms of oppressive hegemony. Within the framework of hospitality, the one who has authority is not the one who speaks in only one voice, but the one who learns to speak in many voices. This model of authority is similar to that assumed by Black feminist bell hooks for whom authority is linked, not to speaking in one ("my/our") distinct voice, but to being able to speak in a "multi-dimensional" voice.[29] Similar to philosophers of language Valentin Volosinov and Mikhail Bakhtin, hooks advocates a shift of emphasis away from authority grounded in consistent and univocal language use (*langue*), to authority grounded in intertextual, interactive, plurivocal, and

---

29. hooks, *Talking Back*, 11–12. According to hooks, "the black poet . . . had many voices—with no single voice being identified as more or less authentic." "The insistence on finding one voice, one definitive style of writing and reading one's poetry, fits all too neatly with a static notion of self and identity that was pervasive in university settings. It seemed that many black students found our situations problematic precisely because our sense of self, and by definition our voice, was not unilateral, monologist, or static but rather multidimensional" (11–12). In many ways this mirrors Bakhtin's "dialogism" in which selves emerge only through complex interactions with others—as sites of struggle, requiring one to engage the heteroglossia within language—"between languages and dialects, between hybridizations, purifications, shifts, and renovations." Bakhtin, "From the Prehistory of Novelistic Discourse," 66. According to Bakhtin, "only polyglossia fully frees consciousness from the tyranny of its own language and its own myth of language," 61.

co-inventive speech (*parole*).[30] Hospitality encourages what Africana philosopher Paget Henry calls a "creolization" that invites the mutual co-optation of an oppressor's speech, the reversal of words from negative to positive meanings, coining new words and phrases to meet emerging situations, and forms of rhetorical invention that make possible the redemption of speech at the interface of differences.[31] Hospitality also encourages homiletical "re-mixing," in which elements from the lives of different people are re-mixed to invent new artistic patterns of thought and action.[32] Authority in this context is a function of one's ability to shape and nurture a community of co-creative, plurivocal redemptive speech.

Third, authority within the framework of hospitality does not become non-assertive, non-resistive, and relativistic. Assertion and resistance, however, are focused primarily on protecting the welcome space (household) and the rights of the guest in relation to that space. In the first instance, the preacher is a steward of the household of faith. Within the codes of ancient hospitality, the host is responsible to the household for its safety and well-being. The host is responsible for maintaining and protecting the mysteries of faith,

30. See Volosinov, *Marxism and the Philosophy of Language*. Volosinov argued, against Ferdinand De Saussure, that "signs are social phenomena living on the boundaries between individuals; and they are meaningful only in the context of social relations among people." Cited in McNally, *Bodies of Meaning*, 112.

31. Henry, *Caliban's Reason*, 88. For a fascinating study of Paul's idea of reconciliation as "Creole consciousness" see Bond, *Paul and the Religious Experience of Reconciliation*.

32. See Leary, "'When We Remix … We Remake!!!'"; Shiga, "Copy-and-Persist"; and Gibson, "God's Little Toys." For a theology commensurate with this idea, see Min, *The Solidarity of Others in a Divided World*.

the scriptures, and the welfare of the household of faith. Yong points out that in the New Testament the rules of hospitality included testing the stranger. This involved ascertaining a stranger's name (is this who he/she really is?), and determining the guest's intentions (does this person intend evil?).[33] According to Christine Pohl, "Boundaries are an important part of making a place physically and psychologically safe."[34] And as Hans Boersma asserts, "Hospitality is an art that is impossible to practice when we refuse to challenge evil."[35] Hospitality is leavened, therefore, with expectations that guests will provide adequate self-disclosure and even penance where required.

This "testing" of the guest's identity and intentions is not, however, a doctrinaire practice rooted in fixed theological dogma or the community's preferences and prejudices. Rather, as Yong points out, discernment is a profoundly improvisational and flexible spiritual practice, a search for a rough "fittingness" to the good news of the gospel. According to Yong, this resembles the discernment of tongues amid the cacophony at Pentecost.[36]

33. Yong, *Hospitality and the Other*, 123–26. This is a significant departure from Derrida's unconditional or pure hospitality in which one must even welcome the devil. For an important outline of this view, based on the eschatology of Ireneaus, see Boersma, "Irenaeus, Derrida and Hospitality."

34. Pohl, *Making Room*, 140; quoted in Yong, *Hospitality and the Other*, 123.

35. Boersma, *Violence, Hospitality and the Cross*, 35; quoted in Yong, *Hospitality and the Other*, 124.

36. Yong relates this flexibility and improvisation to speech act theory and Austin's notion of the felicitous or "happy performance" of religious language within a particular situation. Vanhoozer calls this "dramatic fittingness." See Yong, *Hospitality and the Other*, 54. See also Vanhoozer, *The Drama of Doctrine*, 254–61.

Beyond protecting the welcome space by testing the guest, the host must also protect the safety and voice of the guest. Welcoming the guest requires careful attention to issues of power, inequality, and negative "othering."[37] Letty Russell points out that a "just hospitality" is aware that those who may seem to "fit" could be merely fitting to the church's "superior middle," an exclusionary consensus that stymies the careful discernment of God's open, eschatological welcome of new, life-changing words into the community.[38] The host has a prophetic responsibility, therefore, to help the community remain constantly aware of the potentially dominating aspects of testing the stranger. The host remembers that listening to different voices is more than discerning a canonical fit, or a liberal, multicultural process aimed naively at "harmony and joyful learning."[39] Rather, it is a process that involves power, domination, and the struggle for voice and a place at the koinōnia table. When this struggle is not recognized or is silenced, it is possible, and even desirable, for the guest to rebuke the host. As we noted before, Jesus rebukes his hosts when their practices of testing the stranger reflect an inhospitality that silences the voices of God's prophets (Luke 11:37–51).

Fourth, although prophetic and pastoral assertion is sometimes required to protect the community or to insure "just hospitality," assertion is never allowed to rigidify and become a part of a fixed hierarchy of voiced protector and voiceless beneficiary. Pastoral assertion occurs within an ethos and ethic of hospitality that refuses to communicate to

37. See Sadler, "Can the Cushite Change His Skin?"

38. Russell, *Just Hospitality,* 101–24.

39. For more on this, see Henry Giroux's critique of multiculturalism in education in Giroux, *Border Crossings,* 89–90.

guests that prophetic and pastoral discernment comes *always* and *necessarily* from a fixed mouthpiece. Hierarchy within the framework of hospitality is, as Letty Russell puts it, always "temporary inequality."[40] Whereas the ordained preacher is "above" others as host of the household, he or she also becomes guest when hosted by the spiritual wisdom of strangers within and beyond the household. There is a constantly shifting asymmetry of "above" and "below," or "teacher" and "learner," "preacher" and "congregation" within the host-guest relationship. The preacher as host and guest is eager to learn from God-beloved strangers within a constantly shifting hierarchy of teaching-and-learning in which strangers can be "above" the preacher, bringing special knowledge to the preaching task.

The radical nature of this process and its theological significance should not be missed. The potentially dangerous "omni-power" kenotically "emptied" in this process *is the power to designate who is "other" or who in fact the stranger is*. Without naively losing sight of the "superior middle," and the dynamics of power and struggle involved in establishing voice for many strangers, the preacher in this model does, in reality, de-center and become *guest*. Similar to what occurred at Emmaus in the breaking of bread, it is precisely when *this* reversal occurs that a new, life-giving "word" can be recognized.

Fifth, hospitality has the potential ultimately to shift the locus of authority in preaching away from *both* host and guest toward the great *subject* that is *between* both parties relationally. The truth we are pursuing as preachers gains more authority as we welcome one another in its search. What is

40. Russell, *Growth in Partnership*, 37.

being encouraged here is not "listener-centered," but "subject-centered" preaching. In his book *The Courage to Teach: Exploring the Inner Landscape of a Teacher's Life*, religious educator Parker Palmer unfolds the inner workings of communal epistemology within "the community of truth."[41] The hallmark of the community of the truth, according to Palmer, "is in its claim that *reality is a web of communal relationships, and we can know reality only by being in community with it*."[42]

At the heart of the community of the truth are what Palmer calls "great things." For Christian preachers, these great things include the various dimensions and characteristics of the gospel. The community of truth gathers around these things and holds an "eternal conversation about things that matter, conducted with passion and discipline."[43] The preacher hosts this conversation, not to water down the gospel or search for a lowest common denominator message, but to pursue more of the truth of the gospel than can be otherwise known.

The Basic Practice: Asking Before or During Preaching

Although hospitality in preaching might benefit from a range of practices, one practice in particular is fundamental: "asking" others before or during preaching. As we have observed, the preacher as host and guest does not assume that he or she can identify with another person's experience of the gospel. Because of this, the preacher feels compelled at every turn to *ask*. This is not a general asking that devolves from broad

41. Palmer, *The Courage to Teach*, 90–92.

42. Ibid., 95.

43. Ibid., 104.

assessments of one's pastoral experience, but is a specific asking that *occurs within the context of the preaching task itself*, within the experience of preparing to speak, and/or while delivering the sermon.

Many homileticians have begun to incorporate diverse practices of specific, hospitable "asking" into their homiletical models. Some do this in consultative ways, inquiring about certain social locations and identities. Kathy Black, in *A Healing Homiletic: Preaching and Disability*, is concerned that we ask persons with disabilities for wisdom, especially as we interpret and preach biblical texts about blindness, healing, and leprosy. Christine Smith, in *Preaching as Weeping, Confession, and Resistance: Radical Responses to Radical Evil*, encourages us to ask those who have been victims of handicappism, white racism, classism, ageism, sexism, heterosexism, for wisdom before preaching. In *Telling the Truth: Preaching about Sexual and Domestic Violence*, a range of writers encourage preachers to ask victims of sexual and domestic violence for wisdom before preaching texts about forgiveness, lament, the atonement, *kenosis*, and the family.[44] Nora Tubbs Tisdale, in *Preaching as Local Theology and Folk Art*, encourages congregational ethnography and a thick description of a congregation's local theology before preaching. Sally A. Brown, in *Cross Talk: Preaching Redemption Here and Now* encourages us to ask context-specific questions about the nature of God's saving work in our midst before determining appropriate metaphors for the atonement. In *One Gospel, Many Ears: Preaching for Different Listeners in the Congregation*, Joey Jeter and Ronald Allen encourage preachers to become attuned to differences

---

44. McClure and Ramsay, eds., *Telling the Truth*.

shaped by generation, gender, culture, learning style, social class, and political persuasion in congregations.

Some homileticians are more direct and collaborative in nature, inviting others into actual practices of sermon preparation or delivery. In *The Roundtable Pulpit: Where Preaching and Leadership Meet*, I encourage preachers to include laity in the process of sermon brainstorming in order to welcome the range of voices in and around the congregation into sermons. Charles Campbell and Stanley Saunders in *The Word on the Street: Performing the Scriptures in the Urban Context*, encourage preachers to engage those who live on the streets before preaching sermons that confront the principalities and powers in the urban context. Doug Pagitt, in his book *Preaching Re-imagined: The Role of the Sermon in Communities of Faith*, invites a questioning and consultation of listeners during the practice of preaching itself. Lillian Daniel, in *Tell It Like it Is: Reclaiming the Practice of Testimony* supports the revival of testimonial practices in the church as a way to bring other voices into the pulpit.[45] These and other approaches to homiletics are incorporating this one essential element of a homiletic of hospitality: asking before or during preaching.

The Emergent Word and Wisdom of God

For the preacher as host and guest, the word and wisdom of God are disclosive, not conclusive. They are emergent communal and public realities, arriving through the ongoing give-and-take of open communal and public conversation about the meaning of the gospel in today's world. God's word and wisdom are in process and emerge through ongoing interac-

45. See also Rose, *Sharing the Word*.

tion between scripture, tradition, and multiple experiences of strangers. This process is persuasive, but not in the usual sense. Persuasion is *communal* and *interactive*, an effect or byproduct of people *talking themselves into being Christian.*[46]

This does not mean that the word and wisdom of God are tentative or soft-spoken. A word that is open and in process is not a word whispered. Within a conversation focused on discerning the "great subject" at hand, once that subject is discerned in some aspect, it can and should be proclaimed with as much power and vigor as possible, and in a way that represents the dynamic fashion in which that truth emerged in the host-guest relationship. This is the only way to honor the emergent power and eschatological force of the word and wisdom of God.

AN IMAGINATIVE EXERCISE

I would like to end with a small imaginative exercise along the lines of a guided meditation. Become for a moment the preacher as host and guest. Imagine that in your preaching you are hosting a conversation every week in which there is a great subject in your midst. The context for the conversation you are hosting does not have an entirely clear inside or outside, a sacred centre or a profane margin. You have a fluid sense of your congregation and choose to call it the "community of truth." You are becoming aware of God-beloved strangers of all shapes and sizes coming and going in this community: at home, in the public square, the marketplace,

46. For more on this idea in relation to congregations as "organizational" and "talking" cultures, see my book *The Roundtable Pulpit*, 49–50.

and in your church. Each of these strangers potentially bears witness to a new aspect of the gospel. Some of these strangers knock at the front door of your enlarged church, some simply show up unannounced, others are on the way out. Some seem locked away behind smiles and handshakes—selves hidden beneath roles and rituals, others are "in the closet." Some are alone, some are with many friends. Some are rich, some poor, some older, some younger. There are people of all races and ethnicities. All have infinitely mysterious lives.

On behalf of the safety and well-being of this expanding community of truth you feel compelled to ask names, search out motives, and discern the intentions of the strangers you meet. At the same time, you are aware of how issues of power—often focused on race, ethnicity, class, and gender have led to ongoing exclusion, and you work hard to keep the boundaries of the community open and welcoming.

The expanding sanctuary walls in your imaginative church are increasingly populated with pictures of friends and strangers, relics of mission projects, newspaper clippings, mementos, local artwork, finger-paintings, and reminder notices. The Lord's Table is more like an ordinary table, and it is set in many contexts—wherever a table becomes a "welcome table." The everyday dishes are out, mixed in with the good china. The computer is online, perhaps to receive the testimonies of witnesses elsewhere, in China, Ethiopia, Brazil, or Chile.

Sermon preparation has become portable. Pieces of it take place in a conversation about a biblical text at someone's home, or in a similar conversation at a shopping mall or coffee shop the next. You feel that what you preach on Sunday mornings is connected to and flows from conversations and little proclamations given and received. You don't feel the need to prepare sermons in a church office amid your clerical commentaries. You venture out to other rooms in the church and beyond, to the homes of others, to conversations with lay folks and with people beyond the church—even non-believers, seekers, agnostics, sinners. You still enjoy your clergy lectionary study group but you also want to seek out the spiritual wisdom of many others. You still enjoy rummaging through your commentaries and theology books, but you find yourself saving money and purchasing a broad mix of commentaries and theological resources, lining the shelves with books that bring other perspectives—gendered, racial, ethnic, global— inviting many into the homiletic conversation. Your theology feels dynamic and constantly developing. You find yourself re-thinking the nature of sin, grace, and salvation every day though engagement with strangers.

Before long, you want to place hospitality more formally at the center of your congregational and communicational leadership. You want your preaching to become a *model* of expansive hospitality situated at the center of the church's communicational life—as a pattern for life together in the household of faith. You decide to form a sermon brainstorming group that includes ordinary people of all ages, races, shapes and sizes. Every week you meet with this group in different places: the women's shelter, the men's shelter, the public library, the local school, in front of the local munitions factory or military post, at the nursing home, at the zoo, in the botanical garden, in the youth room at church, in the church basement where the janitor hangs up the brooms. Sometimes the group meets in the homes of different people in the group to think through sermon ideas: a gay couple's apartment, an empty nester's house in the suburbs, an urban community center. You don't want this group to become an exclusive "in-group" so you see to it that the group changes every three or four months. When one member leaves the group, they tag another stranger to take their place. You encourage them to tag someone who has not been heard from—from another neighborhood, race, religion, country, generation, class, or political party. You want them to invite strangers in the midst of the church, strangers even among those we think we know, strangers who have dropped through or dropped out, whose lives have never been consulted as authoritative witnesses to the gospel, never been welcomed into worship or preaching. You also develop contemplative practices in which you seek out and become aware of strangers within yourself you've been avoiding or denying, so you can engage them within the community of truth.

In order to "ask" more broadly, you decide to send out interviewers or "theo-ethnographers" with recorders or cameras to ask people what they hear in our sacred texts. You are amazed at what you hear, and use their proclamations in worship services. When you prepare sermons, you make use of the ideas, emphases, rhythms and logic of what you hear: sometimes an argument, sometimes a clarification, sometimes the striking of a bargain, the listing of complaints, the sharing of fears, the quivering articulation of rage. You no longer feel limited to formal logic: deduction or induction. You become passionate about discovering new forms of logic for preaching that occur in real conversations about God. When standing in the pulpit or talking to a gathering you see not only the faces in front of you, but the mysterious depth behind each face, a depth that is beyond all control which reminds you of the journey you are on—the wild adventure of encountering faith in the company of strangers. This inspires you with the realization that you can never exhaust the search for God's presence, wisdom, and word. In your mind's eye, if not literally, you see your preaching ministry as an ever-expanding roundtable, a place where there is no first and no last, no inside and no outside but a never-ending host-guest conversation in pursuit of God's wisdom and word.

7

Preacher as One "Out of Your Mind"

ANNA CARTER FLORENCE[1]

[1]About that time King Herod laid violent hands upon some who belonged to the church. [2]He had James, the brother of John, killed with the sword. [3]After he saw that it pleased the Jews, he proceeded to arrest Peter also. (This was during the festival of Unleavened Bread.) [4]When he had seized him, he put him in prison and handed him over to four squads of soldiers to guard him, intending to bring him out to the people after the Passover. [5]While Peter was kept in prison, the church prayed fervently to God for him. [6]The very night before Herod was going to bring him out, Peter, bound with two chains, was sleeping between two soldiers, while guards in front of the door were keeping watch over the prison. [7]Suddenly an angel of the Lord appeared and a light shone in the cell. He tapped Peter on the side and woke him, saying, "Get up quickly." And the chains fell off his wrists. [8]The angel said to him, "Fasten your belt and put on

1. A version of this essay first appeared as "Out of Your Mind" in *Journal for Preachers* 28.4 (2005) 36–39.

your sandals." He did so. Then he said to him, "Wrap your cloak around you and follow me." ⁹Peter went out and followed him; he did not realize that what was happening with the angel's help was real; he thought he was seeing a vision. ¹⁰After they had passed the first and the second guard, they came before the iron gate leading into the city. It opened for them of its own accord, and they went outside and walked along a lane, when suddenly the angel left him. ¹¹Then Peter came to himself and said, "Now I am sure that the Lord has sent his angel and rescued me from the hands of Herod and from all that the Jewish people were expecting." ¹²As soon as he realized this, he went to the house of Mary, the mother of John whose other name was Mark, where many had gathered and were praying. ¹³When he knocked at the outer gate, a maid named Rhoda came to answer. ¹⁴On recognizing Peter's voice, she was so overjoyed that, instead of opening the gate, she ran in and announced that Peter was standing at the gate. ¹⁵They said to her, "You are out of your mind!" But she insisted that it was so. They said, "It is his angel." ¹⁶Meanwhile Peter continued knocking; and when they opened the gate, they saw him and were amazed. ¹⁷He motioned to them with his hand to be silent, and described for them how the Lord had brought him out of the prison. And he added, "Tell this to James and to the believers." Then he left and went to another place. (Acts of the Apostles 12:1–17)

Do you ever get the feeling that there are some things about the disciples that maybe we *don't* want to know?— such as: what is this connection with Peter and servant girls? Why, at the tensest moments, is it always the maid who identifies him?

I can think of at least three of these women. There's the servant girl of the high priest, on the night Jesus was arrested: she can identify Peter. She stares at him warming himself by the fire, in the high priest's courtyard, and finally says, "I know you. You were with that Galilean"—which Peter famously denies. There's a second servant girl, according to Matthew, who sees Peter on the porch the same night; she remembers him, too. She tells the people around her, "This man was with Jesus of Nazareth"—which Peter denies again, without bothering to disguise his Nazareth accent. And then a year or so later there's Rhoda, or "Rosie," if you want a loose translation of the Greek: Rosie the maid, from Acts 12.[2] She doesn't even need to *see* Peter in order to recognize him; she knows what he *sounds* like. So when she hears his voice at the door on a night that just happens to be Passover, just like the night when Jesus was arrested, she is so happy she doesn't even stop to open it and rushes to announce to everybody that Peter is at the gate!—which *Peter* doesn't deny, this time, but everyone else does. (*Flip* goes the story . . .) Three servant girls, three denials, three positive ID's.

Now, I realize three instances do not necessarily constitute a trend, and I don't want to make too much of this. There could be a lot of reasons why Peter made such a lasting impression on female domestic staff. Maybe he was exceptionally kind to them. Maybe his sermons promised them a freedom they didn't know in this world. Maybe Peter just stood out from the other disciples because he was the cute one, or the clumsy one, or the one with fisherman's biceps or

2. With thanks to Justo L. González, who, upon hearing that I was working on an Acts 12 sermon about Rhoda, remarked, "Rhoda? Oh—you mean Rosie the maid!"

a Sean Connery Galilean accent; who knows? There could be any number of reasons why these women could identify Peter in the dark, most of which are far too boring to make it into a supermarket tabloid.

For a while I read this story thinking that if those servant women remembered Peter, it must be something about *him*. I suppose I wanted Peter to be the hero; I wanted him to be an unforgettable role model, a caring pastor, a great preacher, a man of the people, a champion of justice, honest and wise and brave and true. I wanted to find us a good preaching role model. And Peter *is* a good one, in this story. Imagine "preaching as Peter": the kind of sermon that people actually notice, because it's not only exegetically sound and contextually sensitive, it's *true*, and even *dangerous*; and I don't mean because Mr. and Mrs. So-and-so will be so mad about what you said that they'll withdraw their money; I mean the kind of dangerous that goes beyond local church politics, so that there are FBI agents sitting in the back pews taking notes, and your sermons are quoted in the *Washington Post*, launching movements, inspiring activists, horrifying the Pentagon, until finally the president himself has no choice but to order your arrest, because your preaching is toppling governments. Can you even picture that?! And imagine, the night before your trial, locked in your cell, guards on either side, alarm systems at every door, and suddenly, an angel appears, breaks your chains, takes your hand, leads you out, and you find yourself free, free to preach another day!

I *love* reading the story that way. Imagine: the preacher who tells the truth, makes a difference, goes to jail, and then, is rescued by angels! Wow. The sermons I would preach, if I thought it would go like that. The things I'd say, on behalf of justice, if all I had to worry about was the Pentagon. No more pressure to keep Mr. and Mrs. So-and-so happy. No more budgets. Just truth . . . and angels. Preacher heaven.

So this is a preaching book, and I admit I got a little carried away thinking about Peter and his angel. I got a little stuck in that reading of the text. I started to believe it was all about *him*: that if Rosie the maid and the other servant girls insisted that they remembered Peter, it must be something about *him*—clearly, his unforgettable preaching. Because that would make a good, inspiring story for us, right? *Be like Peter. Truth . . . and angels. Go in peace.*

But I forgot. Peter isn't the real preacher in this story. Oh, he's a preacher all right, but he isn't doing it right now; he isn't preaching *here*, in this text. The one who *is* preaching, is Rhoda; Rosie the maid. *She's* the preacher. Which might lead us to wonder if our next homiletical hero, our next role model, is Rosie the maid.

The thing about Luke is, he's too careful a writer to leave anything to chance. Every word choice is deliberate and loaded. And when he repeats a particular verb or image, you have to assume that it isn't just by accident; he's trying to make a point. Those word repetitions are like little neon signs in the middle of the text: ****Pay attention.**** *Pay attention.**** That's how I discovered that Rhoda wasn't the only servant girl around: I hauled out my concordance, and there they were, the maid by the fire and the maid at the door, blinking *** at me. But it was the *verbs* that turned this text around for me, all these obscure lexicon parallels between Luke and Acts that only a preacher could love—like did you know, for example, that the word Luke uses for "recognizing" (as in, Rosie the maid *recognizing* Peter) is the same word he uses in the Road to Emmaus story, when Jesus took the bread, and broke it, and their eyes were opened and they *recognized* him?! It's a rare verb for Luke; he doesn't use it much. Or how about this one: the word for what Rhoda does when she recognizes Peter, the word *apaggellō*, that gets translated here as "announced" (as in, "she ran in and *announced* that Peter was standing at the gate")—well, *that* happens to be the same verb John uses in the resurrection story, when Mary Magdelene *announces* on Easter morning, "I have seen the Lord!" Rhoda is the first woman to claim *that* verb since Mary. Is that awesome, or what?!

Sometimes we are allowed one digression into language technicalities; this is my one allotment for the day. Because this is *big*. Luke is telling us, in his very sneaky Lucan way, that Rhoda ran into that room with an *announcement*, a *proclamation*, that *Peter was alive*. He wasn't in jail, the way he was supposed to be; he wasn't dead, the way Herod promised he would be, first thing tomorrow; no, he was alive, and he was standing right outside the gate, because Rhoda heard him knocking, and her ears were opened and she recognized him! (Is this ringing any bells for you, people? I hope so, because Luke is not the least bit subtle about any of this!) *Peter is not dead*, Rhoda announces; *he is alive, and he is here, and I tell you,* she insists, *I heard him!* And you know what? Every single one of those believers, who had spent hours praying for this very thing to happen, every single one of them looked at Rhoda and said, "You're out of your mind." Which isn't quite as rude as telling her that her story is an idle tale and a lot of hogwash, but close.

She proclaimed something, and they didn't believe her. She preached good news, and they dismissed her. *Poor Rhoda. She's out of her mind. She wants Peter back so badly she's start-*

ing to hear things. She announced that the very thing they had prayed for had come to pass, and they told her she was delusional. Why *is* that?!

Do you think she just wasn't convincing enough? Did her announcement lack passion and a depth of personal commitment? Maybe she hadn't adequately grasped the pastoral context, felt their pain, addressed their needs. Maybe she wasn't a very good storyteller: her delivery lacked a certain polish, an awareness of the importance of dramatic structure. Maybe she didn't lean hard enough on the biblical and theological foundations of her message; she should have cited more theologians and scriptural references, argued her case. Maybe she hadn't spent enough time on her focus and function statements. Or maybe her announcement just wasn't very interesting, compared to their prayers. But surely, there must have been *something* she could have done to improve her proclamation and make them believe her. Isn't that what we preachers do, when no one jumps up to believe us? We figure, *Well, it must be me.* Right?

Thank God we have this story. Praise God for Rosie the maid. You know what I hear from her? I hear that a preacher isn't the one who's most convincing; a preacher just has to be convinced herself. A preacher is just the one who recognizes the dead man at the door, and announces to everybody that he's really alive, and he's asking to come in, so shouldn't they go open the gate, now? That's a preacher: a doorman who keeps looking for dead people. A maid named Rosie, who knows Peter's voice when she hears it.

I haven't tried this out on my students yet. You can let me know whether it would have sent *you* round the bend, when *you* were in seminary, to hear that a preacher is really a doorman for dead people, or a doorman who keeps looking for people and things we thought were dead. Things that others tell you are utterly impossible, like ending a war. Things other folks have given up on long ago, like a church that welcomes everyone. Things we pray for, but certainly don't expect to happen, like Peter escaping from Herod. Things no one in this world, no one in their right mind, would dare to hope for.

And that's really it, isn't it? To preach, you can't be in your right mind. You have to be a little out of it, to be perfectly frank. Because there isn't anything that's going to dislocate you more than the grace of God. It will pick you up out of your ordered life, where you pray for the power of God to break into our reality, and it'll do just that: it'll break into any reality you ever thought you had a handle on, and plunk you down on another planet. It will dislocate you until you're out of your mind (wherever that was) and instead, wandering around someplace called the realm of God. Totally illogical. And then you get the call to preach, right?—so God says, "Okay, here's what I want you to do: just wait at the door, and when someone knocks, figure out who it is and then come tell us"—which sounds simple enough until you realize that you're going to spend the rest of your life recognizing the risen Christ and announcing that there's a person we all assumed was dead waiting at the door, and guess what?—*they're not dead now.*

Luke says the other people in the house were amazed, when they finally came to the door and saw Peter. They were *more* than amazed, actually; they were scared witless, scared out of their minds. They were confused and displaced and beside themselves—take your pick, the word means all those things. It's a word Luke uses a lot, maybe because it's a frightening place, the realm of God. It's a frightening thing to see the power of God moving in our very prayers. Little girls we thought were dead turn out to be only sleeping. Paralytics pick up their beds and walk. Women run back from a graveyard with news about an empty tomb. The good news we hoped for really comes to pass, and it scares us to death. I don't blame Peter's friends for choosing to believe in the realm of Herod, where might makes right and prisoners stay put in their cells. I don't blame Peter's friends for telling Rosie the maid she was out of her mind. They were already moving on with their grief. And then her words yanked them right back to that weird, liminal space where miracles aren't just stories you tell about events that happened to someone else; they happen to *you*. It's pretty darn scary, to have to live like that; as though preachers were really telling the truth about who was knocking at the door.

I should probably come clean and tell you that "Rhoda" also means "clown," which has all sorts of familiar implications for preachers: "the clown of God," and so on. But today, I wanted to give you Rosie the maid. I think I prefer her to the clown, actually. I prefer the preacher who's a doorman for dead stuff. It helps me remember that in the end, it's not about me, and my preaching abilities, and never was. *It's about being out of my mind.* Isn't that kind of comforting?—to know that we can't preach at all until we're out of our minds. We can't preach at all until we've spent time as a doorman, or as Rosie the maid, waiting at the gate of the realm of God, paying attention to who knocks, and then running to announce what we've seen. And if it takes a really long time for the people to believe us, well, did you notice that Peter just keeps knocking? Where else is he going to go?

Don't worry about the words. It's enough to be overjoyed by what we've seen and heard in this text, and what we believe about it. Just keep watching. Just keep watching.

8

Preacher as One Entrusted

ROBERT STEPHEN REID

IT IS not particularly difficult for a preacher to invite people to live into the gospel implications of a text like 2 Thessalonians 3:13: "Brothers and Sisters, do not weary in doing what is right." Who could question the value of such a request? It is, however, a bit more complicated when we realize that this gnomic assertion is the final summary affirmation of Paul's concern about how to respond to idlers in the congregation in 2 Thessalonians 3:6–14. From his response it appears that a number of Thessalonican Christians no longer believed that they had to participate in the activities of daily routine, possibly because they were awaiting the return of the Lord or possibly because they believed they were above such concerns as spiritual people. The result was that they had become dependent on the beneficence of others in the congregation while quite probably looking down on their benefactors as somehow less holy for lacking their spiritual commitment.

We would hope that anyone preaching this text today would avoid directing Paul's claim that "Anyone unwilling to work should not eat" at welfare recipients, at people struggling with unemployment, or even at people from other cultures who do not assume our Puritan work ethic. Actually, preachers might be more apt to see modern parallels with the religious "busybodies" who always seem willing to serve at the church's spiritual beck and call even when it is at the expense of family, friends, and work. Beyond the immediate exegetical concerns of interpretation, preaching a text like this provokes questions for everyone about the balance we choose to strike between the spiritual and the physical dimensions of our lives. If we envision our task as preaching intentions aligned with the intention of the text, how does the preacher avoid the claim to do "what is right" to the other without trying to be at lest a bit persuasive or at least suggestive about how to live in a way that balances the physical with the spiritual?

By now, anyone who preaches will have already begun to think of ways to apply Paul's admonitions about work and its relationship to faith—perhaps even to the point of looking up the passage to clarify aspects of what Paul wrote about *busybodies*. And this is my point. From the outset, preaching has always been a matter of trust—trust the congregation has that the individual appointed to interpret God's Word for them will be faithful to God and faithful in their efforts to preach sermonic intentions aligned with scriptural intentions that direct listeners to be people of faith. This conception of *trust* suggests we believe a preacher is doing "what is right" when she or he invites or even calls for our response to live into the claims of the gospel.

PREACHING FOR RESPONSE

In 1958 H. Grady Davis wrote, "The aim of preaching is to win . . . a response to the gospel, a response of attitude and impulse and feeling no less than of thought."[1] This notion of 'winning a response' is still at the heart of most textbooks for public speaking even as some feminist rhetoricians have begun to propose the notion of creating a "collaborative invitation" through speech.[2] Richard Shell and Mario Mousa, the directors of the Wharton Business School's "Strategic Persuasion Workshop" recently proposed *The Art of Woo* as an alternative to trying to persuade by "winning."[3] Why woo? Perhaps because this word, as old as Middle English, evokes the notions of courting another—the efforts of one person to seek the favor of another whether in love or in affairs of the court. Far from thinking of influence as a coercive or combative strategy of communication, most of us probably smile at the idea of being woo'd. If someone is trying to woo us we generally assume that they will try to influence us in ways that are interpersonally sensitive with a goal of receiving our favor. From wining to wooing; clearly a shift appears to be afoot in the metaphors communication theorists are using to think about efforts to influence others.

Given this shift we should not be surprised that homileticians had already begun feeling the need to rethink the

1. Davis, *Design for Preaching*, 5.

2. For example, "Invitational Speaking" is Cindy Griffin's proposal for a new way of designing response into public address; Griffin, *Invitation to Public Speaking*.

3. Shell and Moussa, *The Art of Woo*, 1. Shell and Moussa are the Directors of the Wharton School's Strategic Persuasion Workshop for managers and other business leaders.

role of persuasion in preaching. By the mid 1980s a variety of strategies of preaching to achieve different responses had emerged.[4] In fact, advances in homiletics over the last two decades have been directed toward arriving at new metaphors to reframe a preacher's understanding of and the assumptions about how to evoke an appropriate desired response from listeners. For example:

- Ronald J. Allen views preaching as a "conversation"

- Brad Braxton views preaching as "faithful reporting"

- Walter Brueggemann views preaching as de-centered, re-imaginative "testimony"

- Jana Childers views preaching as Incarnational "performance"

- Richard Lischer views preaching as "Spiritual formation"

- Tom Long views preaching as "witness"

- Christine Smith views preaching as "weaving," as "weeping," as "confession," and as "resistance"

- John Stott views preaching as "bridge-building"

- Paul Scott Wilson views preaching as an "event" of encounter with God.

Each of these metaphors matter because they frame and reveal how this individual understands the intersection between the

4. See Eslinger, *A New Hearing*. Eslinger recently revised and reconceived this work to address the changes of two decades of homiletic practice; Eslinger, *The Web of Preaching*.

divine and the human, the intersection between theology and rhetoric in preaching.

What has remained the same for preaching across the centuries is the interest in influencing a desired outcome. The metaphors may shift but shaping "what to say" and 'how to say it' with a view to achieving a desired response from the congregation has been at the heart of Christian preaching since Justin Martyr first described the practice of house church worship about AD 150. Following the reading of Scripture by a lector, he tells us, the presiding elder then gave "an address urgently admonishing his hearers to practice these beautiful teachings in their lives."[5] Notice that the concern here, like the concern of Paul as he addressed new believers in mission congregations, was that listeners personally enact the teachings as a result of having heard the homily or the teaching. One of the earliest characteristics of Christian *parenesis* is that, unlike the Jewish synagogue practice of expounding the holy laws of scripture point by point, Christian elders exhorted followers to live into the claims of faith.[6] The practice

5. Justin Martyr, *First Apology*, c. 67.

6. In defending the hypothesis that the concept of *faith* in the New Testament should be distinguished from the Hebrew concept of *trust* (i.e., that the notion of *faith* in the Christian Scriptures does not have its origin in Hebrew religion) James Kinnevy argues that the Greek word for faith (*pistis*) entailed 1) the possibility of uncertainty in which assent to belief can occur, 2) the concept of free decision in conversion, and 3) the possibility of an extrinsic cause of belief. He concludes that "The word *pistis* (and its derivates), as it is used in the Christian Scriptures, meant, at least partially, what the word meant in its typical Greco-Roman use: persuasion in the rhetorical sense" (*Greek Rhetorical Origins of Christian Faith*, 135); to have faith in something is to have become persuaded in the plausibility of some set of extrinsic claims as worthy of belief. Kinneavy argues that theologians have been disinclined

of designing an address to seek a response arose as an artifact of urban civilization. The oratorical influence in Christian preaching would come later with the development of preaching as an *art*, but the desire to frame discourse with a goal of seeking an appropriate response to a *homily* has been with us from the beginning. This desire of a speaker to seek a faith-centered response from listeners is what distinguishes this kind of speech from a Christian talk or a conversation about Christian matters.[7]

The metaphor that controls my own understanding of preaching, the trope by which I seek to express the divine-human interplay between divine purposes and human hopes in preaching, is to understand that I serve as 'one entrusted' to seek a response from others. From the beginning of the Christian movement elders in the congregation have understood a significant part of their appointed purpose to be that of mediating divine intentions revealed in the interpretation of biblical texts with those whom they hope will "practice

---

to make this association because they have been loathe to associate such a noble ideal as *faith* with the language of ancient rhetoric—an art that had, until recently, been disparaged by most classicists as unworthy of serious consideration and had been in general disrepute since the Enlightenment (143).

7. On 'exhortation' as intrinsic to the homily from its earliest manifestations see Siegert, "Homily and Panegyrical Sermon," 421–43. Siegert notes that "proclamation" must be distinguished from the sermon and the homily because the former has no rhetorical dimension but was associated with "blowing a trumpet." Ancient trumpeters were not considered musicians, because their practice did not interpret music "any more than heralds interpreted a message." There is no art to heralding and the only response it seeks is attention (426–27). On the effort to identify the constituent elements of a contemporary Christian discourse see Reid, "A Rhetoric of Contemporary Christian Discourse," 109–42.

these beautiful teachings in their lives." It has been a role of trust—the preacher serving as one entrusted to help those who hear homilies live faithfully and the preacher as one entrusted to communicate the claims of the gospel to seekers so that they might become passionate followers of Christ's way.

At this point we might rightly ask, what part in this seeking a response is played by "wooing" and what part is played by "wonder" (at the grace of God)? If *response* is at the heart of preaching, and has been from the beginning of the Christian movement, how are we to understand the relationship between the work of God's grace and the work of the human communicator's craft? What, if anything, is the role of persuasion in preaching? And what do questions about the role of rhetoric and the role of grace have to do with the idea that preachers may want to approach their homiletical task with the assumption that they serve as *one entrusted*? Good questions. I want to take them up briefly before looking at the Biblical and theological sense of considering the preacher as one entrusted.

Is There Still Room for Rhetoric?

It's not difficult to find contemporary homileticians who object to idea that persuasion should play any role in preaching. For example, Tom Long notes, "It is characteristic of more recent homiletics to view persuasion in terms of manipulation and, thus, as a negative characteristic when applied to preaching."[8] Lucy Rose wrote, "I am uncomfortable with [a] continued use of the word 'persuasion' to describe preaching's purpose and ecclesial leadership. Persuasive preaching and leader-

8. Long, *Witness*, 257 n. 6.

ship styles have been abusive to many in the church whose experiences and convictions have been consistently ignored or dismissed . . . [C]ontinued use of the word is potentially dangerous in sanctioning previous definitions and practices."[9] Fred Craddock agrees that contemporary homileticians have come to question the idea whether persuasion should have any place in preaching, but this fact leads him to conclude that, "*Any consideration of the use of rhetoric [in preaching] must first deal with the prior question of persuasion.*"[10] His reason? "Anyone entering the preaching ministry needs to ponder the fundamental question of what one wants to have happen during and after a sermon."[11] Couched carefully in this invitation is a keen awareness that a listener's response is not something that occurs only in a sermon's closing "appeal." Rather, response is constantly implied *during* the sermon as the listener follows the preacher's presentation of ideas.

Craddock is quite right here. We must deal with the prior question of persuasion if we are to arrive at a helpful metaphor that frames a trope that will shape our purpose in preaching. So, how have we come to think of persuasion as something disconnected from reasoning in preaching, as something that only occurs in the sermon's "application" rather than as response that occurs throughout the sermon?[12] A little history can help.

9. Rose, *Sharing the Word*, 133. Rose's perspective is deeply shaped by the work of feminist theologian Catherina Halkes at this point.

10. Craddock, "Is There Still Room for Rhetoric?" 69 (italics original).

11. Ibid., 69.

12. Aristotle devoted most of his treatise on *Rhetoric* to reasoning meaningful for listeners that balances appeals to rationality, to passions, and the listener's perception of the speaker's good will. He employed

This separation of persuasion from reasoning arose in part as an artifact of the Enlightenment and the age of scientific reasoning that tried to separate facts from beliefs. For example, John Whately, the pre-eminent British rhetorician at the outset of the nineteenth century had argued that reasoned arguments and their arrangement should be separated from persuasive appeals to the passions (feeling, sentiment, and emotion). [13] He treated persuasion as an appeal by which a speaker seeks to influence an individual's *will*—a division that goes back to Francis Bacon's definition, "The duty and office of Rhetoric is *to apply Imagination to Reason* for the better moving of the will."[14] John Broadus, the author of the most influential homiletics textbook written in the last 200 years, followed Whately in this matter and specifically relegated persuasion to the "application" portion in a sermon. He wrote, "The chief part of what we commonly call application is *persuasion*. It is not enough to convince men of truth, nor enough to make them see how it applies to themselves,

---

the term *enthymeme* to describe this kind of reasoning distinguishing it from logical reasoning because it always entailed an implicit appeal that seeks a response from the listener. It is distinguished from logical reasoning that always seeks valid conclusion through a conclusive demonstration. In addition to these implied appeals that occur in most talk, we now think of everyday reasoning as shaped by the *exigencies* of the situation that calls forth the communication as a reasonable response, the *constraints* of what would make the talk reasonable in that situation, and the nature of the *audience* from whom a speaker's talk seeks a response. This kind of contingent reasoning, which calls on people to make choices and reflectively engage ideas, relies on probabilities rather than certainties. See Corbett, *Classical Rhetoric for the Modern Student*, 59–66; Lucaites and Condit, "Introduction," 1–18.

13. Whately, *Elements of Rhetoric*, 282.

14. Bacon, "The Advancement of Learning," 743.

and how it might be practicable for them to act it out—but we must 'persuade men.'"[15] This separation of persuasion from reasoning intended to influence listeners is still held by many homileticians long after those same homileticians have rejected Broadus's approach to homiletics.

This view that persuasion represents an appeal to a person's *will*, while reasoning about convictions is somehow separate from any persuasive activity, has not held up over time. Few communication theorists since Perleman and Olbrecht-Tyteca presented a case that argument's purpose is to gain the "adherence of minds" would treat reasoning primarily as logical or "rational" argument to the exclusion of persuasion.[16] In 1963, argument theorist Stephen Toulmin shifted treatment of what he called "sound argument" away formal assumptions of rational validity to the standard of whether an argument "will stand up to criticism." Today, almost all university students are taught how to analyze argument and reasoning by identifying Toulmin's way of categorizing its claims, its data, its warrants, its backing, and its conclusions—the sum of which can lead a person to be *persuaded* by sound reasoning.[17] A third significant rhetorician from this same period, Kenneth Burke, argued that rhetorical motives are not captured best in the Machiavellian paradigm so aptly explored in *The Prince*. He turns, instead, to another book from the same period by Baldassare Castiglione titled *The Book of the Courtier*. If *The Prince* represents the definitive work on how to maintain power over others, *The Book of the Courtier* was the definitive

15. Broadus, *On the Preparation and Delivery of Sermons*, 232.
16. Perelman and Olbrechts-Tyteca, *The New Rhetoric*.
17. Ibid., 8; Toulmin, *The Uses of Argument*, 8.

work on how to court the assent of people of influence and how to court the assent of people whose favor is sought.[18]

Professor Rose understandably expresses frustration over the view that persuasion in preaching can too often become a *Machiavellian* rather than a *courtly* enterprise. Others who have sought to explore metaphors for preaching like conversation, testimony, and spiritual formation are similarly uncomfortable with conceptions of preaching that tend to provide *de facto* answers as God's truth rather than exploring in a more nuanced fashion the larger theological question of how any of us are to understand our identity as the people of God for this time and this place. But we all do well to follow Craddock's call to come to terms with the "prior question of persuasion" in preaching. For without an understanding of

18. Burke is more interested in wooing than winning, since he believes it is the primary task of a communicator to establish rapport by way of identification with the audience (*A Rhetoric of Motives*, 46). On his exploration of courting and *The Book of the Courtier*, see Burke, *A Rhetoric of Motives*, 221–33. This view of persuasion as courting assent by "wooing" rather than "winning" is also at the heart of the ancient Platonic dialogues about rhetoric as well. The difference between an informative speech and a persuasive speech is not whether there is an effort to influence. The issue is whether there is an element of controversy. Informative speeches still seek to woo listeners even if they do not propose any alternatives to be overcome. Many homileticians understandably reject the idea that preaching should begin with a controversy while others have become concerned with privileging one view or one voice over others. But since Watzlawick, Beavin, and Jackson wrote *Pragmatics of Human Communication* it has been difficult to suggest that a person speaking to another or others can avoid influencing the other any more than a person cannot not communicate. It is not surprising that many homileticians would reject the idea that the purpose of preaching is to win assent. On the other hand, the idea that preaching (as well as testifying) still seeks to *woo* those who "have ears to hear" is a notion deeply embedded in the biblical tradition.

the role of persuasion it is almost impossible to arrive at an ethic of responsible preaching. I have explored a typology of what I have termed irresponsible preaching practices that can arise when preachers fail to develop a healthy understanding of persuasion in preaching elsewhere.[19] But I suspect we have all seen or heard of instances where an inadequate theology of homiletic persuasion has turned into a lack of respect for listeners through failures of inauthenticity, greed, and exploitation of others, or in a lack of faithfulness to the gospel through failures of self-absorption, trendiness, and self-righteousness in presuming to have all the answers.

Is there still room for rhetoric? The tendency to want to see ourselves rise above the use of such a potentially problematic art has always been with the church. But rather than adopting either a naïve view of persuasion or an either/or way of thinking, we do well to ask ourselves how a responsible approach to persuasion will play a part in the way we preach.[20]

Does Admitting Room for Rhetoric Crowd Out Grace?

Recently James Kay and William Willimon have questioned whether homileticians have placed too much emphasis on rhetoric to the exclusion of concern for theology and God. Kay believes theologians should clarify their presuppositions

19. Robert Stephen Reid, "Irresponsible Preaching."

20. In discussing objections by other homileticians to the rhetorical orientation of David Buttrick, Richard Eslinger concludes that such individuals seem to be suggesting that, "the only way to avoid manipulating—or brainwashing—the congregation is for the preacher to remain naïve about language's function in oral communication within the assembly"; Eslinger, *The Web of Preaching*, 195.

about poetics and rhetoric before engaging in discussions about method and practice. Willimon believes that attending to issues of rhetoric and listeners places too much focus on the human element of preaching with the often unintended consequence that God ceases to be the subject matter of the testimony. Whenever rhetoric dominates theology these concerns are surely right.

The question of preaching's starting point matters because where one starts tends to control the trajectory of what one sees. If a preacher begins with the concerns of rhetoric then the primary concern of preaching likely will be *effectiveness* and the distinctiveness of the Christian message as testimony about God and God's purposes will be lost. Concern over starting points and "grounding" can become equally problematic, however, if it becomes an excuse for an idealism that suggests concern for *response* is irrelevant, or worse, irreverent. The latter is the equivalent of stressing the revelatory quality of the Incarnation to the exclusion of its ontological reality, of stressing the miraculous nature of the Incarnation to the exclusion of its functional purpose. Reducing the role of rhetoric and the concern for the listener in preaching to an 'either/or' forced choice between the efficacy of the work of the Holy Spirit vs. the efficacy of human craft turns an ancient debate over agency into a duel that, at its historic best, has always been resolved in favor of a 'both/and' solution (e.g., Augustine).[21]

In delivering the inaugural address on his appointment as the Joe R. Engle Professor of Homiletics and Liturgics at

21. My argument here develops claims made in Reid, "Rhetoric—Introduction," 345. The claim that we must resist the either/or approach in homiletics is articulated well by Long in his seminal essay, "And How Shall They Hear?" 178.

Princeton Theology Seminary, James Kay took the opportunity to lay challenge to American preaching's historic reliance on rhetoric. Kay surveys this history questioning whether theories of eloquence are adequate to express divine truth. At issue, he argues, is not "How to preach?" Rather, the question is "What is preaching?" Following Karl Barth and in opposition to the dominating influence of nineteenth-century homileticians who saw preaching as a branch of rhetoric, Kay argues that preaching must first be understood as a subfield of dogmatics and that its frame of reference needs to be shifted from agency to purpose. Where some critics have suggested that a Barthian homiletic drives "a stake through the heart of rhetoric," Kay maintains that what Barth rejected was "an autonomous rhetoric theologically ungoverned, that claims for eloquence the power to make God real for people."[22] What matters for Kay is the question of whether one can mistakenly assume *agency* for rhetoric that theology reserves to God alone. Barth, he concludes, would argue that "Any persuading that may occur, or any 'enlightening' that is a saving illumination, can only be attributed to the divine Speaker and that of hearing the Word of God wrought by the Holy Spirit."[23]

For this reason, preaching for Barth, should be an effort to recreate for contemporary listeners the witness of scripture's own testimony of the divine—to reframe the divine rhetoric that performs Gospel. Preaching that reduces scripture to a source of religious ideas to be synthesized as a big idea, as something to be rendered in points, as a theme to be developed by a law-gospel/problem-solution design, or one of the many other strategic organizational designs mistakenly places

22. Kay, "Reorientation," 22; cf. *Theology*, 34–37, 39–40.

23. Kay, "Reorientation," 23; See Barth, *Homiletics*, 104.

a humanly devised means of agency over that of the design of the Biblical testimony. As Kay presents the argument, the question is about the frame of reference a preacher employs that structures how proclamation of Scripture's testimony will be approached. If the preacher begins by attending to rhetoric rather than theology, then the proclamation is never Word of God because it originates from a human concern for communicating with listeners rather than a divine regard to be testimony concerning God. In an effort to affirm a rhetoric that begins with the right starting place he states,

> I offer the following thesis: *Preaching is more faithful to the Word of God when it is fitting or appropriate to its hearers' context.* One possible way to defend this thesis is by means of the concept of *concursus*, that is, the "concurring" or "accompanying" of divine and human action, traditionally associated with Lutheran and Reformed doctrines of providence. As recently interpreted by Christopher Morse, *concursus* [implies that] ... "God's providing is always custom made to fit the creaturely recipient so that the creature's own freedom is never abrogated but activated."[24]

Hence, the work of sermon-crafting, when theologically authorized by the doctrine of *concursus*, can provide preachers with a means to be faithful to the Word of God while offering a "fitting or appropriate" witness adapted to the needs of listeners.[25] The role of rhetoric is thus implied by this doctrine, but never to be assumed as its starting point.

---

24. Kay, "Reorientation," 33 (citing Morse, *Not Every Spirit*, 293); cf. Kay, *Theology*, 57.

25. Kay, "Reorientation," 34; cf. Kay, *Theology*, 58.

I am persuaded by the basic concern of this argument. Preachers must begin development of a sermon from a theologically grounded perspective both in their homiletic exegesis and in their understanding that grace as a response to the preached word is a work of God rather than something controlled by rhetorical design. But rather than turning to a doctrine of *concursus*, I draw on the Pauline conception of preaching as a partnership with the divine (2 Cor 6:1), a serving as *one entrusted* where agency is shared as a *trust* between God and the preacher and between the preacher and those with who the testimony is shared. I believe that testimony that names God and names grace, to truly be testimony, must be offered in some form of human partnership with God or the term testimony ill-befits the reality that it is a person who is testifying.[26] If any response to testimony is all grace and with no admittance to a role for craft, then testimony ultimately fails the test of being a divine-*human* witness. I do not fully confess to understand how it is that a Christian sermon offered as Word of God can be both fully God and fully human testimony to God. But, like the Incarnation, I affirm that it is both possible and that it serves as a very pale but very real testimony to the human-divine Incarnation itself.

William Willimon will have none of this. There is no concession to rhetoric; not even a doctrine of *concursus*. In *Conversations with Barth on Preaching* he summarizes Barth's epistemology by stating, "He who says 'God' says 'Miracle.'"[27] Only God can speak or testify about Godself. This, for

26. On preaching as "testimony that names God and names grace" see Reid, *The Four Voices*, 21–22.

27. Willimon, *Conversations with Barth*, 127; citing Barth, *The Epistle to the Romans*, 120.

Willimon, is the miracle of the Incarnation to which preachers and believing Christians give witness. He states,

> Though Barth's stress upon the miraculous, gifted quality of Christian communication may seem to some preachers a shaky foundation upon which to build a sermon, it takes off the preacher's shoulders the burden of finding the right words, the right technique, and the right form in order that a sermon "works." It also suggests that some of our sermonic "failures" are due to God and not to us! Preaching is, for Barth, something that God does, a gift. A gift that cannot be withheld is not a gift. It is not our job to make preaching "effective" or "relevant." That task belongs to the Holy Spirit. Jesus Christ is not only the proclaimed but also the Proclaimer, not only the object of revelation but also the revealer.[28]

For Willimon preaching needs to find its way back to its true subject matter rather than take lessons in communicating *effectively*. He maintains that, "Any attempt to be persuasive rests upon the a-theistic assumption . . . that it is up to the preacher to persuade, move, argue, demonstrate, and convince."[29] If preaching begins with concerns of effectiveness and relevance than this assertion is fair. What can be lost

28. Willimon, *Conversations with Barth*, 127–28. In making this claim, Willimon appears to be following Dietrich Ritschl's reading of Barth; Ritschl, *A Theology of Proclamation*. For a significant assessment of Ritschl's role in this debate see Resner, *The Preacher and Cross*, 62–65.

29. Willimon, *Conversations with Barth*, 155. The notion of "reasoning" seems noticeably absent from this list, but if he has reserved it as the descriptor for what preachers do offer in sermons we might rightly ask how he arrives at the distinction between it and the terms he supplies. It would be a slippery slope to defend the difference as one of kind rather than degree. Cf. Willimon, *Proclamation and Theology* and Owens, "Jesus Christ Is His Own Rhetoric!"

in framing the question this way, however, is the classic concern for shaping preaching for a response.

Willimon concedes that there is an intentional circularity to Christian belief that does not need to justify its claims to faith in God or justify the need to make sense of these claims to the world. In such a world, the language of faith is tied to a particular linguistic community. The doctrine of *concursus* is an example of this kind of contextualized theological language that justifies how God can be the sole agent of listener response while in no way delimiting the agency of a speaking human's contribution. Such language is employed primarily to reaffirm the central theological commitments of the community that gave rise to the need to resolve the dilemmas of its own system of thought. The point I wish to make here (and one which Willimon would likely concede) is the fact that its circularity would likely fail to convince anyone who does not share the language commitments of this community—in this case a particular kind of post-liberal theology. Such affirmations tend to be embraced as an argument for constitutive identity within that discourse community rather than as an effort to posit reasoning that would be intelligible to others outside of that community.[30]

30. On this point Willimon believes that preachers must contextualize their message (264), but response should not be their concern. In fact, he concedes in the final pages of *Barth on Preaching* that, released from the constraints of Christendom compromises, preachers are "now free to proclaim the gospel utterly dependent upon God for the reception of the Gospel" (259). As such, "We are stewards not only of the gospel but also the gifts that God has given us—intelligence, voice, physical appearance, personality—and we have a responsibility not to deny or to neglect those gifts but to develop them" (263). In this context note that Willimon prefers the metaphor of "Preacher as Steward" rather than the Barthian trope of "Preacher as Herald" (253).

Thus, I affirm Willimon's assertion that, "The preacher is unable to convert or to persuade anybody. When Preaching 'works,' when it is true, it is testimony to the grace of God, an event of divine election, divine vocation, divine justification, and divine sanctification. Barth's stress on preaching as an exercise of justification by faith links him with Reformation thought on preaching."[31] But that same assertion would not then lead me to affirm, "We can't preach! When preaching works, it is not because I have had good training in homiletics and have used that training well, but rather as an exemplification of the doctrine of justification of sinners."[32] The first assertion is a claim of faith that preaching is an Incarnational event. Yes. The second claim goes further and seems to deny any human quality to Incarnation. If we believe that "in Christ God was reconciling the world to himself, not counting their trespasses against them, and entrusting the message of reconciliation to us" (2 Cor 5:19), then just as the divine was both God and man in the Incarnation, so the message is both God and human in its preaching. For me this is mystery. It is, however, not a justification for an "either/or" approach to answering the question "What is preaching?" I believe in a "both/and" approach which requires that we who preach draw on our best theological understanding in partnership with our best understanding of effective human communication practice in order to be faithful in expressing the message with which we have been *entrusted*. If preaching is a divine-human dance, theology is the partner that must lead. Yet it is also an Incarnational event, which means that the other partner's ability to humanly testify matters. Preaching as one entrusted

31. Ibid., 160.
32. Ibid., 161.

would be without meaning if it is not "*fitting or appropriate to its hearers' context*" and designed to *court* an appropriate response to divine concerns.

HOMILETIC AGENCY AND THE TROPE OF ENTRUSTING

So, if asked to articulate my theology of the mystery of shared agency in contrast to those who would have God alone be the agent in the task of true preaching, I affirm Paul's claim that "in Christ God was reconciling the world to himself, not counting their trespasses against them, and entrusting (θέμενος) the message of reconciliation to us" (2 Cor 5:19). I would merely add that in this declaration I hear a double affirmation of Incarnation. The first is that of the fully divine-human Jesus and the second its continuing echo in the trust implied in the divine-human gospel dance that is preaching as Word of God. The act of 'entrusting' the message (to Paul, in context, and by extension to all others who function as *ambassadors* of this message) translates a word that connotes an act of commitment by God for God's own sovereign purpose.[33] This awareness of shared agency only increases in writings of the late apostolic era (cf. 1 Tim 1:12; *Barnabas* 6:10; 7:11; 9:9).

"Entrusting" (τίθημι) suggests a determination on God's part to share agency with the chosen representative—a "placing" that functions as a trust in the agent to whom responsibility has been delegated to be one who will be faithful

---

33. The word θέμενος is an aorist participle in the middle voice from τίθημι. The word τίθημι means "to place, to set, to commit, etc.," and, in context, can imply "for God's own purpose"; Zerwick and Grosvenor, *Greek New Testament*, 545.

in translating and affecting an understanding of the leader's message/interests with the people to whom she or he serves as an *ambassador*. It is not the task of the *ambassador* to persuade. Rather, as Paul maintains, "So we are ambassadors for Christ, since God is making his appeal through us . . . As we work together (συνεργοῦντες) with him, we urge you also not to accept the grace of God in vain" (2 Cor 5:20—6:1).[34] An ambassador may seek to *court* the favor of listeners, but always with the goal to facilitate a response to the "appeal" (παρακαλοῦντος) that springs from the one with whom she or he works together with.

This rhetorical trope of an ambassadorial identity that occurs in preaching by way of a "working together" with God reflects for me the nature of the partnership, in which an appointed individual does her or his best to represent the interests of and speak testimony on behalf of the One who is served. It is the ambassador's *responsibility* to authentically testify to and serve to the best of her or his *ability* as agent for the divine message and also to court or gain the favor of others concerning the claims and concerns of the One represented. And it is in this second trust—courting the favor of listeners on behalf of the message—that the craft of rhetoric avails. It is in this participation of a *dance* that the divine and human can come together in shared agency in preaching. The responsible preacher seeks to interpret the implied appeal of the text or a claim of a theological conception and convey that interpretation in such a way to court a favorable response from listeners.

34. Paul's use of συνεργοῦντες appears to be an effort to qualify the implications of his use of the middle voice two verses before.

"WHAT HAS JERUSALEM TO DO WITH ATHENS?"

Homiletical agency can be explored by way of a great variety of biblical tropes that provide various representations of individual's struggling to understand what it means to be one called to speak testimony as Word of God. Tropes of homiletical agency, whether by way of concurrence, gift, or entrusting, likely reveal more about the context and the assumptions of the communicator than whether they represent some form of contingent or non-contingent communication.

Though some may wish to point to the Apostle Paul's struggle with those who were rhetorically trained in his day as one of the first to actively reject the role of the rhetoric's "plausible words of wisdom" (1 Cor 2:1–5), we do well to remember that representatives of his Corinthian adversaries were later forced to admit that Paul's "letters are *weighty* and *strong*, but his bodily presence is weak, and his speech contemptible" (2 Cor 10:9–10). A century before, Dionysius of Halicarnassus had already treated the terms translated as *weighty* (βαρειαί) and *strong* (ισχυραί) as formal descriptors of rhetorical *force* in written composition. So Paul's ability to compose formidable prose argument that would be accepted as plausible argument by rhetoricians is not in question.[35] Paul clearly saw it as his purpose to make the claims of gospel intelligible to the communities with whom he corresponded. The either/or urge to reject the rational contributions of of-

35. For discussion of the Dionysian rhetorical references relating to Paul's rhetoric see Reid, "Paul's Conscious Use," 203. For the general state of the art assessment on the debate concerning Paul's rhetorical skill in argument construction see Porter, "Paul of Tarsus and His Letters," 535–36.

fering good reasons concerning the faith actually begins with the third and fourth century church leaders.

Perhaps its first and best-known articulation is attributed to Tertullian, who in the third century posed the following challenge to those willing to baptize "pagan Greek philosophy" *freely* into the Christian worldview:

> What has Jerusalem to do with Athens, the Church with the Academy, the Christian with the heretic? Our principles come from the Porch of Solomon, who had himself taught that the Lord is to be sought in simplicity of heart. I have no use for a Stoic or a Platonic or a dialectic Christianity. After Jesus Christ we have no need of speculation, after the Gospel no need of research. When we come to believe, we have no desire to believe anything else; for we begin by believing that there is nothing else which we have to believe. (*Prescription against Heretics* 7.9)

At issue for Tertullian is really the starting place from which one's thought should proceed. After all, beginning assumptions obviously shape the way questions get formed and, therefore, make all the difference in the possible answers produced. Should we start with faith "believing that there is nothing else with which we have to believe"—the posture classically associated with fideism? Or, should we start with argument, believing that reason matters—the posture classically associated with rationalism? If we pose the question in this way it would seem that our predetermined destination will necessarily proscribe the kinds of questions we ask.

Every generation that would think theologically about faith's reasons and the reasonableness of faith knows this perennial question: "How should the worlds of revelation and reason relate?" Tertullian's reflection on this question, usually reduced to the evocative query "What has Jerusalem to do with Athens?" is often cited in order to disparage any theological use of natural reason. Yet this is an over-reading, since for Tertullian, the question was one of priority rather than of an either-or choice.[36] In the closing words of his delightful treatise *On the Pallium* he returns to the question of the forced option between the two worlds of Christian reflection and classical culture. When challenged as to why he wore the *pallium*, the cloak associated with philosophers rather than the modest toga worn by other Christians, he responded that the humble pallium of the pagan philosopher is ennobled once it is donned by a Christian. He wrote, "All that is liberal in studies is covered by my four angles ... I confer on it likewise a fellowship with a divine sect and discipline. Joy, Mantle, and exult! A better philosophy has now deigned to honour thee, ever since thou hast begun to be a Christian's vesture!"[37]

In our effort to reconcile these worlds as "both/and" possibilities rather than "either/or," we who preach do well to take up Tertullian's mantle. In this way, *rhetoric* and, yes, even persuasion, when it is taken up into and subsumed by a constructive theology of preaching, can become a fitting part of the fabric of the preacher's "Christian vesture" offered as testimony to faith in God. The preacher then need only be faithful to the task with which she or he has been *entrusted*.

Joy, Mantle, and Exult!

36. Cf. Osborn, *Tertullian, First Theologian of the West*, 45.
37. *On the Pallium*, 6.4.

Bibliography

Adams, John Quincy. *Lectures on Rhetoric and Oratory.* 2 vols. 1810. Reprinted, Delmar, NY: Scholars' Facsimiles and Reprints, 1997.

Allen, Ronald. *Interpreting the Gospel: An Introduction to Preaching.* St. Louis: Chalice, 1998.

Attridge, Harold W. *The Epistle to the Hebrews.* Philadelphia: Fortress, 1989.

Auerbach, Erich. *Mimesis: The Representation of Reality in Western Culture.* Garden City, NY: Doubleday, 1957.

Austin, J. L. *How to Do Things with Words.* Edited by J. O. Umson. Cambridge: Harvard University Press, 1962.

Bacon, Francis. "[Excerpt from] The Advancement of Learning." in *The Rhetorical Tradition: Readings from the Classical Times to the Present.* 2nd ed. Edited by Patricia Bizzell and Bruce Herzberg. Boston: Bedford, 1990.

Bakhtin, Mikhail. "From the Prehistory of Novelistic Discourse." In *The Dialogic Imagination: Four Essays,* 41–83. Edited by Michael Holquist and translated by Caryl Emerson and Michael Holquist, 41–83. Austin: University of Texas Press, 1981.

Barth, Karl. *The Epistle to the Romans.* 6th ed. Translated by Edwyn C. Hoskyns. Oxford: Oxford University Press, 1968.

———. *Homiletics.* Translated by Geoffrey W. Bromily and Donald E. Daniels. Louisville: Westminster John Knox, 1991.

Beker, J. Christiaan. *Paul the Apostle: The Triumph of God in Life and Thought.* Philadelphia: Fortress, 1980.

Berger, Klaus, M. Eugene Boring, and Carsten Colpe. *Hellenistic Commentary to the New Testament.* Nashville: Abingdon, 1995.

Black, Kathy. *A Healing Homiletic: Preaching and Disability.* Nashville: Abingdon, 1996.

————. "A Perspective of the Disabled." In *Preaching Justice: Ethnic and Cultural Perspectives*, edited by Christine Marie Smith, 6–25. Cleveland: United Church Press, 1998.

Blair, Hugh. *Lectures on Rhetoric and Belles Lettres*. 1783. Delmar, NY: Scholars' Facsimiles and Pamphlets, 1993.

Block, James E. "National Revival as the Crucible of Agency Character." In *A Nation of Agents: The American Path to a Modern Self and Society*, edited by James E. Block, 369–423. Cambridge, MA: Belknap, 2002.

Boersma, Hans. "Irenaeus, Derrida and Hospitality: On the Eschatological Overcoming of Violence." *Modern Theology* 19 (2003) 163–80.

————. *Violence, Hospitality and the Cross: Re-appropriating the Atonement Tradition*. Grand Rapids: Baker Academic, 2004.

Bond, Gilbert L. *Paul and the Religious Experience of Reconciliation: Diasporic Community and Creole Consciousness*. Louisville: Westminster John Knox, 2005.

Boorstein, Michelle. "Our Father, Who Art in Flagrante: Passion Pics Bestir Celibacy Debate." *The Washington Post*, May 7, 2009. Online: http://www.washingtonpost.com/wp-dyn/content/article/2009/05/06/AR2009050603897.html.

Bornkamm, Günter. "Mysterion." In *The Theological Dictionary of the New Testament*, Vol. IV. Edited by Gerhard Kittel. English version edited and translated by Geoffrey W. Bromiley. Grand Rapids: Eerdmans, 1967.

Bowald, Mark Alan. *Rendering the Word in Theological Hermeneutics: Mapping Divine and Human Agency*. Aldershot, UK: Ashgate, 2007.

Broadus, John A. *A Treatise on the Preparation and Delivery of Sermons*, 2nd ed. Philadelphia: Smith, English, & Co., 1871. Reprint, Dearborn, MI: University of Michigan Historical Reprint Series, 2006.

Brown, Alexandra. *The Cross and Human Transformation: Paul's Apocalyptic Word in 1 Corinthians*. Minneapolis: Fortress, 1995.

Brown, Sally. *Cross Talk: Preaching Redemption Here and Now*. Louisville: Westminster John Knox, 2008.

Brueggemann, Walter. *Isaiah 1–39*, Westminster Bible Companion. Louisville: Westminster John Knox, 1998.

Burke, Kenneth. *A Rhetoric of Motives*. Berkeley: University of California Press, 1969.

———. "The Four Master Tropes." *A Grammar of Motives,* 503–17. New York: Prentice Hall, 1945.

Buttrick, David. *Homiletic: Moves and Structures.* Minneapolis: Fortress, 1987.

Campbell, Charles L. *Preaching Jesus: New Directions for Homiletics in Hans Frei's Postliberal Theology.* Grand Rapids: Eerdmans, 1997.

———. *The Word before the Powers.* Louisville: Westminster John Knox, 2002.

Campbell, George. *The Philosophy of Rhetoric.* 1776. Reprint, Carbondale: Southern Illinois University Press, 1998.

Carroll, Jackson W. *As One With Authority: Reflective Leadership in Ministry.* Louisville: Westminster John Knox, 1991.

Child, Heather, and Dorothy Colles. *Christian Symbols, Ancient and Modern: A Handbook for Students.* New York: Scribner, 1971.

Coakley, Sarah. "Kenosis and Subversion: On the Repression of 'Vulnerability' in Christian Feminist Writing." In *Swallowing a Fishbone? Feminist Theologians Debate Christianity,* edited by Daphne Hampson, 82–111. London: SPCK, 1996.

———. "Kenosis: Theological Meanings and Gender Connotations." In *The Work of Love: Creation as Kenosis,* edited by John Polkinghorne, 192–210. Grand Rapids: Eerdmans, 2001.

Corbett, Edward. *Classical Rhetoric for the Modern Student.* 3rd ed. New York: Oxford University Press, 1990.

Cox, Harvey. *The Seduction of the Spirit: The Use and Misuse of People's Religion.* New York: Simon & Schuster, 1974.

Craddock, Fred. "Is There Still Room for Rhetoric?" In *Preaching on the Brink: The Future of Homiletics,* edited by Martha J. Simmons, 66–74. Nashville: Abingdon, 1996.

Csordas, Thomas J. *Language, Charisma, and Creativity: The Ritual Life of a Religious Movement.* Berkeley: University of California Press, 1997.

Daniel, Lillian. *Tell it Like it Is: Reclaiming the Practice of Testimony.* Herndon VT: Alban Institute, 2005.

Daniélou, Jean. *Holy Pagans of the Old Testament.* Translated by Felix Faber. Baltimore: Helicon, 1957.

Davis, H. Grady. *Design for Preaching.* Philadelphia: Fortress, 1958.

Derrida, Jacques. "Faith and Knowledge: The Two Sources of 'Religion' at the Limits of Reason Alone." In *Religion*, edited by Jacques Derrida, and Gianni Vattimo, 1–78. Translated by David Webb. Stanford: Stanford University Press, 1998.

Dostoevsky, Fyodor. "The Dream of a Ridiculous Man: A Fantastic Story." In *The Best Short Stories of Fyodor Dostoevsky*, 263–85. Translated by David Magarshack. New York: Modern Library, 2001.

Dunn, James D. G. *Jesus and the Spirit: A Study of the Religious and Charismatic Experience of Jesus and the First Christians as Reflected in the New Testament*. 1975. Reprinted, Grand Rapids: Eerdmans, 1997.

Ellingsen, Mark. *The Integrity of Biblical Narrative: Story in Theology and Proclamation*. Minneapolis: Fortress, 1990.

Emerson, Caryl. "Foreword." In Greg M. Nielsen, *The Norms of Answerability: Social Theory Between Bakhtin and Habermas*, ix–xii. Albany: State University of New York Press, 2002.

Eslinger, Richard L. *A New Hearing: Living Options in Homiletical Method*. Nashville: Abingdon, 1987.

———. *The Web of Preaching: New Options in Homiletic Method*. Nashville: Abingdon, 2002.

Evans, Donald D. *The Logic of Self-Involvement: A Philosophical Study of Everyday Language with Special Reference to the Christian Use of Language about God as Creator*. London: SCM, 1963.

Farley, Edward. *Good and Evil: Interpreting a Human Condition*. Minneapolis: Fortress, 1990.

———. *Practicing Gospel: Unconventional Thoughts on the Church's Ministry*. Louisville: Westminster John Knox, 2003.

———. "Preaching the Bible and Preaching the Gospel." *Theology Today* 51 (1994) 90–103. Republished in Edward Farley, *Practicing Gospel: Unconventional Thoughts on the Church's Ministry*. Louisville: Westminster John Knox, 2003.

Farris, Stephen. *Preaching that Matters: The Bible in Our Lives*. Louisville: Westminster John Knox, 1998.

Fénelon, Francçois. *Dialogues on Eloquence*. Edited by Wilbur Samuel Howell. Princeton: Princeton University Press, 1951.

Forest, Jim. *Praying with Icons*. Maryknoll, NY: Orbis, 1997.

Fosdick, Harry Emerson. *The Living of These Days: An Autobiography.* New York: Harper, 1956.

Frank, Thomas. *Business Culture, Counterculture, and the Rise of Hip Consumerism.* Chicago: University of Chicago Press, 1998.

Frank, Thomas, and Matt Weiland. *Commodify Your Dissent: Salvos from the Baffler.* New York: Norton, 1997.

Frei, Hans W. *The Identity of Jesus Christ: The Hermeneutical Bases of Dogmatic Theology.* Philadelphia; Fortress, 1975.

Gibson, William. "God's Little Toys: Confessions of a Cut and Paste Artist." *Wired* Vol. 13.7 (2007) 118–19.

Giroux, Henry A. *Border Crossings: Cultural Workers and the Politics of Education.* 2nd ed. New York: Routledge, 2005.

Gorman, Michael J. *Cruciformity: Paul's Narrative Spirituality of the Cross.* Grand Rapids: Eerdmans, 2001.

Gowler, David B. "Hospitality and Characterization in Luke 11: 37–54: A Socio-Narratological Approach." *Semeia* 64 (1993) 213–51.

Green, Julien. *God's Fool: The Life and Times of Francis of Assisi.* Translated by Peter Heinegg. San Francisco: Harper & Row, 1985.

Griffin, Cindy L. *Invitation to Public Speaking.* 3rd ed. Stamford, CT: Wadsworth, 2008.

Griffin, Em. *The Mind Changers: The Art of Christian Persuasion.* Wheaton, IL: Tyndale, 1976.

Hampson, Daphne. "On Power and Gender." *Modern Theology* 4 (1988) 234–49.

Hengel, Martin. *Crucifixion: In the Ancient World and the Folly of the Message of the Cross.* Translated by John Bowden. Philadelphia: Fortress, 1977.

Henry, Paget. *Caliban's Reason: Introducing Afro-Caribbean Philosophy.* New York: Routledge, 2000.

Hogan, Lucy Lind, and Robert Reid. *Connecting with the Congregation: Rhetoric and the Art of Preaching.* Nashville: Abingdon, 1999.

hooks, bell. *Talking Back.* Boston: South End, 1989.

Horkheimer, Max, and Theodor W. Adorno. "The Culture Industry: Enlightenment as Mass Deception." In *Dialectic of Enlightenment,* edited by Gunzelin Schmid Noerr, 120–67. Translated by Edmund Jephcott. Stanford: Stanford University Press, 2002.

Horner, Robyn. *Jean Luc Marion: A* Theo-*logical Introduction.* Aldershot, UK: Ashgate, 2005.

Hoshor, John P. "American Contributions to Rhetorical Theory and Homiletics." In *History of Speech Education in America: Background Studies.* Edited by Karl R. Wallace, 129–52. New York: Appleton-Century-Crofts, 1954.

Jeter, Joseph R. Jr., and Ronald Allen. *One Gospel, Many Ears Preaching for Different Listeners in the Congregation.* St. Louis: Chalice, 2002.

Jewett, Robert. *Paul: Apostle to America.* Louisville: Westminster John Knox, 1994.

Johnson, Stephen. Apocalyptic *Eschatology as Homiletical Deep Structure.* ThD dissertation, University of Toronto, 2007.

Julian of Norwich. *Showings.* New York: Paulist, 1978.

Kay, James F. *Preaching and Theology.* St. Louis: Chalice, 2007.

———. "Reorientation: Homiletics as Theologically Authorized Rhetoric." *Princeton Seminary Bulletin* 24.1 (2003) 16–36.

———. "Theology of Proclamation." In *The New Interpreter's Handbook of Preaching*, edited by Paul Wilson et al., 493–98. Nashville: Abingdon, 2008.

Kelsey, David. *The Uses of Scripture in Recent Theology.* Philadelphia: Fortress, 1976.

Kiefert, Patrick R. *Welcoming the Stranger: A Public Theology of Worship and Evangelism.* Minneapolis: Fortress, 1992.

Kinneavy, James L. *Greek Rhetorical Origins of Christian Faith: An Inquiry.* New York: Oxford University Press, 1987.

Knowles, Michael P. *We Preach Not Ourselves: Paul on Proclamation.* Grand Rapids: Brazos, 2008.

Koenig, John. *New Testament Hospitality: Partnership with Strangers as Promise and Mission.* Philadelphia: Fortress, 1985.

Koester, Craig R. "Hebrews, Rhetoric, and the Future of Humanity." *Catholic Biblical Quarterly* 64 (2002) 103–23.

Krueger, Derek. *Symeon the Holy Fool: Leontius's* Life *and the Late Antique City.* Berkeley: University of California Press, 1996.

Kuruvilla, Abraham. *Text to Praxis: Hermeneutics and Homiletics in Dialogue.* London: T. & T. Clark International, 2009.

———. "The World in Front of the Text: An Intermediary between Text and Praxis." An unpublished paper presented at the 2008 Society of

Biblical Literature Convention in Boston, MA, in the Homiletics and Biblical Studies section.

Leary, Chris. "'When We Remix . . . We Remake!!!' Reflections on Collaborative Ethnography, the New Digital Ethic, and Test Prep." *Journal of Basic Writing* 26.1 (2007) 88–105.

Lewis, C. S. *The Four Loves.* New York: Harcourt, Brace & World, 1960.

Lischer, Richard. "Preaching and the Rhetoric of Promise." *Word & World* 8 (1988) 66–79.

Long, Thomas, G. *The Witness of Preaching.* 2nd ed. Louisville: Westminster John Knox, 2005.

———. "And How Shall They Hear? The Listener in Contemporary Preaching." In *Listening to the Word: Studies in Honor of Fred Craddock*, 167–88. Edited by Gail R. O'Day and Thomas G. Long. Nashville: Abingdon, 1993.

———. "Authority (Theology)." In *The New Interpreter's Handbook of Preaching*, edited by Paul Scott Wilson et. al., 440–44. Nashville: Abingdon, 2008.

Lose, David J. *Confessing Jesus Christ: Preaching in a Postmodern World.* Grand Rapids: Eerdmans, 2003.

Lucaites, John Louis, and Celeste Michelle Condit. "Introduction." *Contemporary Rhetorical Theory: A Reader*, edited by John Louis Lucaites and Celeste Michelle Condit, 1–18. New York: Guilford, 1999.

Luccock, Halford Edward. *In the Minister's Workshop.* Nashville: Abingdon-Cokesbury, 1944.

Lucian. *On Salaried Posts in Great Houses.* Loeb Classsical Library. Translated by A. M. Harmon. New York: Putnam, 1921.

Malherbe, Abraham. "'Gentle as a Nurse': The Cynic Background to 1 Thess ii." *Novum Testamentum* 12 (1970) 203–17.

Marion, Jean-Luc. *God without Being: Hors-Texte.* Chicago: University of Chicago Press, 1991.

Martin, Luther H. *Hellenistic Religions: An Introduction.* New York: Oxford University Press, 1987.

Martyn, J. Louis. "Epistemology at the Turn of the Ages: 2 Corinthians 5:16." In *Christian History and Interpretation: Studies Presented to John Knox*, edited by W. R. Farmer, C. F. D. Moule, and R. R. Niebuhr, 269–88. Cambridge: Cambridge University Press, 1967.

McClure, John S. *Other-wise Preaching: A Postmodern Ethic for Homiletics.* St. Louis: Chalice, 2001.

————. *The Roundtable Pulpit: Where Leadership and Preaching Meet.* Nashville: Abingdon, 1995.

McClure, John S., and Nancy Ramsay, editors. *Telling the Truth: Preaching about Sexual and Domestic Violence.* Cleveland: United Church Press, 1999.

McFague, Sallie. *Metaphorical Theology: Models of God in Religious Language.* Philadelphia: Fortress, 1982.

————. *Models of God: Theology for an Ecological, Nuclear Age.* Philadelphia: Fortress, 1987.

McNally, David. *Bodies of Meaning: Studies on Language, Labor, and Liberation.* Albany: State University of New York Press, 2001.

Meeks, Wayne A. "Introduction to the WJK edition." In *John Howard Schütz, Paul and the Anatomy of Apostolic Authority,* xxiii–xxiv. 1975. Reprinted, Louisville: Westminster John Knox, 2007.

Melanchthon, Phillip. *Melanchthon on Christian Doctrine: Loci Communes 1555.* Edited by Clyde L. Manschreck. Oxford: Oxford University Press, 1965.

Meyer, Marvin W., editor. *The Ancient Mysteries, A Sourcebook: Sacred Texts of the Mystery Religions of the Ancient Mediterranean World.* San Francisco: Harper & Row, 1987.

Min, Anselm. *The Solidarity of Others in a Divided World: A Postmodern Theology after Postmodernism.* London: T. & T. Clark International, 2004.

Morse, Christopher. *The Logic of Promise in Moltmann's Theology.* Philadelphia: Fortress, 1979.

————. *Not Every Spirit: A Dogmatics of Christian Disbelief.* Valley Forge, PA: Trinity, 1994.

Mosheim, Johann Lorenz von. *Anweisung erbaulich zu predigen.* Edited by C. E. von Windheim. Erlangen: Walthers, 1763. Quoted by Manfred Josuttis, "Homiletik und Rhetorik [1968]." In *Rhetorik und Theologie in der Predigtarbeit: Homiletische Studien,* 9. Homiletische Studien 1. Munich: Kaiser, 1985.

Murav, Harriet. *Holy Foolishness: Dostoevsky's Novels and the Poetics of Cultural Critique.* Stanford: Stanford University Press, 1992.

Murphy, Francesca Aran. *God is Not a Story: Realism Revisited.* Oxford: Oxford University Press, 2007.

Nieman, James R., and Thomas G. Rogers. *Preaching to Every Pew Cross-Cultural Strategies.* Minneapolis: Fortress, 2001.

Nelson, John S. *Tropes of Politics: Science, Theory, Rhetoric, Action.* Madison: University of Wisconsin Press, 1998.

Noll, Mark. *Between Faith and Criticism: Evangelicals, Scholarship, and the Bible in America.* Vancouver, BC: Regent College Publishing, 2004.

Nygren, Anders. *Agape and Eros: A Study of the Christian Idea of Love, Part One.* Translated by A. G. Herbert. London: SPCK, 1932.

O'Connor, Flannery. *Mystery and Manners: Occasional Prose.* Edited by Sally Fitzgerald and Robert Fitzgerald. New York: Farrar, Straus, and Giroux, 1957.

Ogletree, Thomas W. *Hospitality to the Stranger: Dimensions of Moral Understanding.* Philadelphia: Fortress, 1985.

Osborn, Eric. *Tertullian, First Theologian of the West.* Cambridge: Cambridge University Press, 1997.

Owens, L. Roger. "Jesus Christ Is His Own Rhetoric! Reflections on the Relationship between Theology and Rhetoric in Preaching." *Currents in Theology and Mission* 32 (2005) 187–94.

Pagitt, Doug. *Preaching Re-imagined: The Role of the Sermon in Communities of Faith.* Grand Rapids: Zondervan, 2005.

Palmer, Parker. *The Company of Strangers: Christians and the Renewal of America's Public Life.* New York: Crossroad, 1992.

———. *The Courage to Teach: Exploring the Inner Landscape of the Teacher's Life.* New York: Jossey-Bass, 1997.

Papanikolaou, Aristotle. "Person, *Kenosis* and Abuse: Hans Urs Von Balthasar and Feminist Theologies in Conversation." *Modern Theology* 19 (2003) 41–65.

Perelman, Chaim, and Lucy Olbrechts-Tyteca. *The New Rhetoric: A Treatise on Argumentation.* 1958. Notre Dame: University of Notre Dame Press, 1969.

Perkins, Pheme. *Love Commands in the New Testament.* New York: Paulist, 1982.

Peterson, Brian K. *Eloquence and the Proclamation of the Gospel in Corinth.* SBL Dissertation Series 163. Atlanta: Scholars, 1998.

Plato. "*Phaedrus.*" In *Plato, Vol. I: Euthyphro, Apology, Crito, Phaedo, Phaedrus.* Translated by H. N. Flowler. Cambridge: Harvard University Press, 1983.

Pohl, Christine. *Making Room: Recovering Hospitality as a Christian Tradition.* Grand Rapids: Eerdmans, 1999.

Porter, Stanley E. "Paul of Tarsus and His Letters." In *Handbook of Classical Rhetoric in the Hellenistic Period 330 B.C.—A.D. 400,* edited by Stanley E. Porter, 533–86. New York: Brill, 1997.

Randolph, David James. *The Renewal of Preaching: A New Homiletic Based on the New Hermeneutic.* Philadelphia: Fortress, 1969.

———. *The Renewal of Preaching in the Twenty-First Century: The Next Homiletics.* 2nd ed. Eugene, OR: Cascade Books, 2009.

Rees, Elizabeth. *Christian Symbols, Ancient Roots.* London: Kingsley, 1992.

Reid, Robert Stephen. *The Four Voices of Preaching.* Grand Rapids: Brazos, 2006.

———. "Commentary." In David James Randolph, *The Renewal of Preaching in the Twenty-First Century: The Next Homiletics,* 111–35. Eugene, OR: Cascade Books, 2009.

———. "Paul's Conscious Use of *Ad Herennium* Argument Strategies in 1 Corinthians." *Journal of Greco-Roman Christianity and Judaism* 3 (2006) 65–92.

———. "A Rhetoric of Contemporary Christian Discourse." *Journal of Communication and Religion* 31.2 (2008) 109–42.

———. "Rhetoric—Introduction: Seeking a Response." In *The New Interpreter's Handbook of Preaching,* edited by Paul Scott Wilson et al., 343–46. Nashville: Abingdon, 2008.

Resner, André, Jr., *Preacher and Cross: Person and Message in Theology and Rhetoric.* Grand Rapids: Eerdmans, 1999.

———. "Social Justice." In *The New Interpreter's Handbook of Preaching,* edited by Paul Scott Wilson et al., 135–37. Nashville: Abingdon, 2008.

Reumann, John. "'Servants of God'—Pre-Christian Religious Application of the *Oikonomos* in Greek." *Journal of Biblical Literature* 77 (1958) 339–49.

———. "*Oikonomia*-Terms in Paul in Comparison with Lucan *Heilsgeschichte.*" *New Testament Studies* 13 (1966/67) 147–67.

Ritschl, Dietrich. *A Theology of Proclamation*. Richmond, VA: John Knox, 1960.

Rose, Lucy Atkinson. *Sharing the Word: Preaching in the Roundtable Church*. Louisville: Westminster John Knox, 1997.

Russell, Letty M. *Growth in Partnership*. Louisville: Westminster John Knox, 1981.

————. *Just Hospitality: God's Welcome in a World of Difference*. Edited by J. Shannon Clarkson and Kate M. Ott. Louisville: Westminster John Knox, 2009.

Sadler, Rodney S., Jr. "Can the Cushite Change His Skin? Cushites, 'Radical Othering' and the Hebrew Bible." *Interpretation* 60 (2006) 386–403.

Sampley, J. Paul. *Walking between the Times: Paul's Moral Reasoning*. Minneapolis: Fortress, 1991.

Saunders, Stanley P., and Charles L. Campbell. *The Word on the Street: Performing the Scriptures in the Urban Context*. 2000. Reprinted, Eugene OR: Wipf and Stock, 2006.

Saward, John. *Perfect Fools: Folly for Christ's Sake in Catholic and Orthodox Spirituality*. Oxford: Oxford University Press, 1980.

Schneewind, J. B. *The Invention of Autonomy: A History of Modern Moral Philosophy*. Cambridge: Cambridge University Press, 1998.

Schütz, John Howard. *Paul and the Anatomy of Apostolic Authority*. Society for New Testament Studies Monograph Series 26. Cambridge: Cambridge University Press, 1975.

Shell, G. Richard, and Mario Moussa. *The Art of Woo: Using Strategic Persuasion to Sell Your Ideas*. New York: Penguin, 2007.

Shiga, John. "Copy-and-Persist: The Logic of Mash-up Culture." *Critical Studies in Media Communication* 24.2 (2007) 93–114.

Siegert, Folker. "Homily and Panegyrical Sermon." In *Handbook of Classical Rhetoric in the Hellenistic Period 330 B.C.—A.D. 400*, edited by Stanley E. Porter, 421–43. Leiden: Brill, 2001.

Sittler, Joseph. *The Anguish of Preaching*. Philadelphia: Fortress, 1966.

Smith, Christine. *Preaching as Weeping, Confession, and Resistance: Radical Responses to Radical Evil*. Louisville: Westminster John Knox, 1992.

Smith, Ted A. *The New Measures: A Theological History of Democratic Practice*. Cambridge: Cambridge University Press, 2007. 182–220.

Stott, John. *The Preacher's Portrait: Some New Testament Word Studies.* Grand Rapids: Eerdmans, 1961.

Tell, David. "Burke's Encounter with Ransom: Rhetoric and Epistemology in 'Four Master Tropes.'" *Rhetoric Society Quarterly* 34.4 (2004) 33–54.

Tertullian. "On the Pallium." *The Ante-Nicene Fathers* 4. Translated by S. Thelwall. 1885. Peabody, MA: Hendrickson, 1994.

———. "Prescriptions against the Heretics." In *Early Latin Theology: Selections from Tertullian, Cyprian, Ambrose, and Jerome.* Edited and translated by S. L. Greenslade. Louisville: Westminster John Knox, 1996.

Thomas, Frank. *They Like To Never Quit Praisin' God: The Role of Celebration in Preaching.* Cleveland: Pilgrim, 1997.

Thompson, Diane Oenning. "Problems of the Biblical Word in Dostoevsky's Poetics." In *Dostoevsky and the Christian Tradition,* edited by George Pattison and Diane Oenning Thompson, 69–99. Cambridge Studies in Russian Literature. Cambridge: Cambridge University Press, 2001.

Tisdale, Nora Tubbs. *Preaching as Local Theology and Folk Art.* Fortress Resources for Preaching. Minneapolis: Fortress, 1997.

Toulmin, Stephen. *The Uses of Argument.* Cambridge: Cambridge University Press, 1958.

Tracy, David. *The Analogical Imagination: Christian Theology and the Culture of Pluralism.* New York: Crossroad, 1981.

Trenham, Josiah. "Fools for Christ." Online: http://www.saintandrew.net/fr_josiah/homilies/fools_for_christ_pnt8.htm.

Tripolitis, Antonia. *Religions of the Hellenistic-Roman Age.* Grand Rapids: Eerdmans, 2002.

Underhill, Evelyn. *An Anthology of the Love of God from the Writings of Evelyn Underhill.* Edited by Lumsden Barkway and Lucy Menzies. New York: Morehouse-Barlow, 1976.

Vanhoozer, Kevin J. *The Drama of Doctrine: A Canonical-Linguistic Approach to Christian Theology.* Louisville: Westminster John Knox, 2005.

———, editor. *Nothing Greater, Nothing Better: Theological Essays on the Love of God.* Grand Rapids: Eerdmans, 2001.

Volosinov, V. N. *Marxism and the Philosophy of Language.* Translated by Ladislav Matejka and J. R. Titunik. Cambridge: Harvard University Press, 1929.

Watzlawick, Paul, Janet Helmick Beavin, and Don D. Jackson. *Pragmatics of Human Communication: A Study of Interactional Patterns, Pathologies, and Paradoxes.* New York: Norton, 1967.

Weaver, Richard. "The *Phaedrus* and the Nature of Rhetoric." In *The Ethics of Rhetoric*, 3–26. Davis, CA: Hermagoras, 1985.

Weber, Max. *Economy and Society.* Vols. 1–2. Edited by Guenther Roth and Claus Wittich and translated by Talcott Parsons. 1922. Reprint, Berkeley: University of California Press, 1978.

———. *The Theory of Social and Economic Organization.* Translated by A. M. Henderson and Talcott Parsons. 1947. Reprinted, New York, Oxford University Press, 1964.

Whately, Richard. "*Elements of Rhetoric.*" In *The Rhetoric of Blair, Campbell, and Whately*, edited by James L. Golden and Edward P. J. Corbett, 273–399. Carbondale: Southern Illinois University Press, 1990.

Wheeler, Sondra. *What We Were Made For: Christian Reflections on Love.* San Francisco: Jossey-Bass, Wiley & Sons, 2007.

White, L. Michael. "Social Authority in the House Church Setting and Ephesians 4:1–16." *Restoration Quarterly* 29 (1987) 209–28.

Willimon, William H. *Conversations with Barth on Preaching.* Nashville: Abingdon, 2006.

———. *Proclamation and Theology.* Horizons in Theology. Nashville: Abingdon, 2005.

Willimon, William H., and Stanley Hauerwas. *Resident Aliens: Life in the Christian Colony.* Nashville: Abingdon, 1989.

Wilson, Paul Scott. *The Four Pages of the Sermon.* Nashville: Abingdon, 1999.

———. *The Practice of Preaching.* Nashville: Abingdon, 1995.

———. *Preaching and Homiletical Theory.* St. Louis: Chalice, 2004.

———. *Setting Words on Fire: Putting God at the Center of the Sermon.* Nashville: Abingdon, 2008.

Wilson, Paul Scott, Jana Childers, Cleophus LaRue, and John Rottman, editors. *The New Interpreter's Handbook of Preaching.* Nashville: Abingdon, 2008.

Witherspoon, John. "Lectures on Eloquence." In *The Selected Writings of John Witherspoon*, edited by Thomas Miller, 231–318. Carbondale: Southern Illinois University Press, 1990.

Wolterstorff, Nicholas. *Lament for a Son*. Grand Rapids: Eerdmans, 1987.

Wren, Brian. *What Language Shall I Borrow? God-Talk in Worship*. New York: Crossword, 1989.

Wright, Wendy. "Fools for Christ." *Weavings: A Journal of the Christian Spiritual Life* 9 (Nov/Dec 1994) 23–31.

Wuellner, William H. *The Meaning of "Fishers of Men."* New Testament Library. Philadelphia: Westminster, 1962.

Yong, Amos. *Hospitality and the Other: Pentecost, Christian Practices, and the Neighbor*. Maryknoll, NY: Orbis, 2008.

Zerwick, Max, and Mary Grosvenor. *A Grammatical Analysis of the Greek New Testament*. Unabridged and rev. ed. Rome: Biblical Institute Press, 1981.

Index